The second half of life

A Woman's Road to Inner Wisdom

Marina Oppenheimer, LMHC

**The second half of life
A Woman's Road to Inner Wisdom**

© 2014 Marina Oppenheimer, LMHC
All rights reserved
Published in the United States of America
Ediciones Horizontales Co.
First Edition March 2015
ISBN-13: 978-1-68086-028-3
ISBN-10: 1-68086-028-3

To my beloved son Thomas,
My link to Transcendence ...

Table of Contents

ACKNOWLEDGEMENTS

I would like to acknowledge the many authors I have read in my life and whose philosophies and views of the world have shaped mine. I also want to thank all my patients for sharing with me their more intimate stories, as well as my friend Lawrence Kulenkamp for his excellent suggestions.

All names have been changed to protect privacy

I remember reading a long time ago that we all have one life problem to solve but that it takes us a long time to identify it. While the luckiest among us are able to understand what this problem is during this lifetime, many of us are unable to even know where to start looking. When I read that book (I totally forgot its title) it was many years ago and the statement seemed to me a little simplistic. Just one life problem? Life is full of issues, I thought. How can all of our life struggles end up being just one? At that time of my life I was so immersed in my daily family responsibilities that I soon forgot all about it. Years went by and soon enough life changed its path to enter into that difficult stage called *The Empty Nest Syndrome.* My son left for college, my now ex-husband moved to a new house, and I was left with no options but to gather the broken pieces and move on. Or so I thought. When I started reading all the books I could find on how to start a life after divorce at middle age, they all pointed to the fact that life has a lot to offer and that after working on my grief I should be able to start anew. However, I could not really grasp the meaning of *starting anew*. No matter how you look at it, the pain of divorce after many years of marriage is so deep that trying to put it behind us is just an illusion, like those mirages that appear to the stranded desert traveler. It was only several years later that I realized that my grief was not there to be forgotten but to be remembered, to be kept in a present state of mind so as to understand its meaning, a meaning that had probably to do with the one life issue I needed to face. Not at all like the man who had lost the keys to his house and was looking for them far away from the door. When a neighbor came by and asked him if he had dropped the keys at that spot, the man said that he had dropped them near the door but that he was looking for them under the lamppost because the light was much brighter there. This man was looking for an easy way out of darkness. Unfortunately, understanding the meaning of the experiences that come our way is all but easy. This brings to mind the famous but enigmatic saying "Know Thyself" from the Delphi Oracle. Understanding ourselves will not be a matter of walking a new path or reinventing our lives but, on the contrary, of staying on the same course and learning the lessons we need to learn; especially regarding those issues that are similar in nature and that keep happening to us over and over again. If the same problem keeps repeating itself under different disguises it's because there is something that needs to be changed for us to evolve to a higher plane. Otherwise we will stay stuck in the same place until we learn the lessons we came to this life to learn. Fortunately, we have our dreams to help us in this difficult task of understanding who we really are. True, dreams are obscure; but if we take the time to write them down as soon as we wake up and we analyze them with care, gradually their meaning will become apparent. I believe that the most important thing to bear in mind is the fact that there is more to life than meets the eye. *"Life is a Dream"* says Calderon de la Barca alluding to the fact that we human beings are not really in touch with our true Selves. If we knew our Selves more deeply, our relationships with ourselves and with others would certainly be more genuine and real communication would be possible. In my

specific case it took me several years to finally see the light at the end of the tunnel. I still remember what one of the therapists I went to see after my divorce said to me after our first session: "Since childhood you seem to have played the role of the pleaser. It is obvious that you have not shed this role in adulthood and as long as you keep being a people pleaser you will attract to your life people who need to be taken care of." The implication was obvious: I had chosen to take care of others to make sure that they loved me, a behavior learned during the first years of my life. Until one day something magic happened: I made an unconscious choice that would change my life forever. I stopped pleasing others and put myself first. That was the beginning of my road towards individuation. If I wanted to change I needed to take care of myself and have others like me for who I am and

not for what I can do for them. Not an easy task to say the least, but I am gradually achieving this goal. In other words: I am learning to establish healthy boundaries in my relationship with the world. Needless to say, because of this change many ties that I thought were unbreakable broke. It was a necessary step for me to become me. These *Necessary Losses** became the hero hurdles in my voyage towards wholeness. So I thanked all my nemeses and I let them go, not without wishing them the best for having being my teachers in this journey called Life. These nemeses were the signs sent to me by the Universe to alert me about the things that I needed to work on. Now that their mission has ended, in my middle age years I am ready to embark in a new journey of discovery.
Wish me luck!

* *Necessary Losses* by Judith Viorst

ALL OF THE UNHAPPINESS OF MAN STEMS FROM ONE THING ONLY: THAT HE IS INCAPABLE OF STAYING QUIETLY ALONE IN HIS ROOM.

B. PASCAL

In one of my blog posts on the empty nest syndrome I stressed the importance of using our free time to learn. I believe knowledge is what will help us regain balance by providing us with a vital goal after our children are gone: understand what we need to change in ourselves to become better human beings. This is exactly what I had prescribed Claudia after her last child left for college. Claudia was one of those very intelligent women who would have excelled as a professional but decided instead to dedicate most or her time to raising her three children. Hers had been a lifelong investment in her family well-being. Although she had graduated with a degree in computer science and managed to hold several part-time jobs while the children were young, her profession had not been her priority. Those of you who read my blogs probably know already how this story ended, so the fact that *husband left after last child went to college* should not come as a surprise. That had happened some four years ago, but despite my suggestions, Claudia was still at a loss about what to do with her life.

"I feel as if I had been fired from a company for which I worked for twenty some years" she said during a session. "I feel anxious and with the need to run from one activity to the next."

Claudia was unable to concentrate and as a result she could not read, enroll in a course, update her resume, or look for a job. The only thing she could do was planning things to do with her friends every day of the week. Needless to say, not only was she spending a lot of money but also her anxiety level would only decrease if she had company. Coming home after a date was like coming back to jail. Although on the surface Claudia seemed to be having a good time, she knew well that life was not supposed to be lived on the streets. Her intuition told her that she still had to process the loss she had gone through and that meant that she had a lot of issues waiting to be addressed. I told Claudia that we needed to establish a treatment goal.

"We will know that therapy was successful if the following goal is achieved: being able to feel comfortable when alone at home," I suggested. She agreed, although she did mention at the time that such a goal seemed insurmountable.

"Why don't we start by analyzing Pascal's statement: "*All the unhappiness of man stems from one thing only: that he is incapable of staying quietly alone in his room*?" I said to her one rainy afternoon as we were starting the session. I remember thinking that the weather was well suited for our topic.

"What does it mean to you that happiness has to do with being able to sit quietly in your room?" I asked my patient.

"I don't know what to say because I am unable to do it. When I am alone in my house I feel like the walls are closing in on me," she added nervously.

It was obvious to me that I had pushed a delicate button. Claudia went on: "When I come back home the walls seem cold and sweaty like those of an abandoned house."

"Perhaps yours is an abandoned house, "I agreed. "After all you are never there."

I could sense my patient's anxiety level rising, so I decided to take the lead. There are situations when I feel that the person sitting in front of me is standing at the edge of a cliff and that I need to facilitate some of the work.

"Our house is one of our mirrors," I said. "When we are unable to be at home alone what it means is that we are unable to be alone with ourselves. In our solitude there is no avoiding or escaping what has to be revisited and changed."

"But I don't really miss my ex-husband. What I miss are my children," said Claudia almost in tears. "My loneliness stems really from my children being away," she went on. "I am not grieving my marriage. I swear."

"I hear you," I said. "Being a mother myself I know exactly what you mean when you say that your grieving is about your children having left home and about you entering a new life stage." I waited for a moment to see if Claudia would expand on this issue, but she remained silent. She seemed to be desperately looking for guidance.

"I believe that there is only one way to face life crises, especially at middle age," I went on. "However the task is not an easy one." Still not a word from my patient, who looked at me as if waiting for some secret formula that would ease her pain. "You will have to trust Life and accept that your pain was necessary," I said looking at her intently. To say that Claudia was taken aback by my words would be an understatement.

"Wait, let me explain," I said." Pain is our path towards wisdom. Pain is evolutionary in the sense that it allows us to become wiser and stronger. Pain is our link to the Universe because it allows us to understand what it means to be human."

"You mean that it makes us more humble?" asked Claudia.

"That too," I said. "But what is really important is that our suffering in this life is the suffering we have chosen to suffer in order to learn what we came to learn."

Claudia looked at me with sudden interest.

"But what did I come to learn?" she asked.

"That you will have to find out," I retorted somewhat enigmatically. "And what a better place to do that than in the solitude of your own room?"

IF WE FEEL LONELY WHEN WE ARE WITH OURSELVES IT'S BECAUSE WE ARE IN BAD COMPANY.

J.P. SARTRE

I started thinking about the real meaning of loneliness after so many of my patients came to see me complaining about it. True: we all feel lonely once on a while, but what struck me as strange was that many of my patients, although they had a satisfactory social life, could not avoid feeling that they were not really connected to their surroundings. One of them described her feelings as a sort of depersonalization. Sabina was a 62 year old widow mother of two grown sons who had left the family home several years ago. One of them was married with children, while the other son was single and living in a different state. Sabina had a good relationship with her married son as well as with her daughter-in-law, so much so that she visited them and her grandchildren regularly. Her relationship with the other son was also good, but she saw him less often. She also had a nice group of friends, mostly women her own age who were also widowed or divorced, as well as some married friends with whom she met often for dinner and the movies. Her life seemed to flow peacefully if it weren't for a strange sense of isolation that sometimes pervaded her for no apparent reason. At those times, Sabina felt that she desperately needed to be with someone to talk about her feelings, although it was difficult for her to confess that she felt so deeply alone. Sabina had already visited another therapist to find out how to overcome her emotional isolation, but the practical recommendations given to her –stop your negative thoughts, get busy, travel, take a course- had not helped her. So she decided to ask a friend to recommend another clinician. That is how she came to my office.

"I came to ask you a very specific question," she said. "I want to get rid of my sense of isolation. It's ruining my life," she added. Sabina asked me this question after having told me that her life did not lack anything, except of course a partner with whom to share the good and the not so good. However, her life experiences had taught her that having a partner is not a guarantee against loneliness. Furthermore, Sabina had decided that being middle aged she preferred to live alone, so as not to share all her time and space with somebody else. Loneliness is a fact of life. Sabina already knew that. What is not supposed to be a fact of life is the sense of not belonging anywhere, of being lost in the dark. Like Sartre artfully wrote, being with ourselves shouldn't necessarily be bad company. However, dealing with these feelings is anxiety provoking and we all tend to overcome them by keeping busy. But busy is not really the answer to loneliness. The answer lies somewhere else, deep down within ourselves, and we need to access our Self in order to find it.

"The easy road to overcome isolation is finding a companion with whom to share our life," I said. "But you have already discarded that option."

"Exactly," she answered. "I would like to live alone and still be OK with myself. What I would like is to shed that feeling of void that sometimes fills my heart. Do you think it's doable or does it pertain to this stage of life to feel that way?"

"As we all know, loneliness is a part of life at any stage. No one is exempt from loneliness at one time or another," I explained.

Loneliness is a complex topic even for us therapists because, as I said before, it is easy to fall into the trap of suggesting easy solutions. Since approximately 27% of the US population lives alone, we therapists need to become creative in addressing the subject of isolation so as to find a way to help our patients make use of their aloneness in a positive way. As in many other situations, I started thinking about my own aloneness and how I face it.

"One thing is certain," I started saying. "Human beings are sociable beings. We need others to feel good about life. However, that does not mean that we have to be with others all the time and that we cannot at times be alone with ourselves," I added.

Sabina looked at me anxiously waiting for what would come next. I took some time to think about how to describe my thoughts in a way that would make sense to her. Most of all I wanted to avoid giving her a one size fits all formula because I know that we human beings fight our demons in very different ways.

"When we are alone and we are confronted with our isolation, we need to reframe our thinking pattern from "*I am totally alone*" to "*What do I need to learn from this situation?*" I stopped to check if Sabina was following me. She was.

"I know what you mean, but although the words sound beautiful I still don't understand how to put them into practice," was her answer.

"OK, I am going to share with you my own way of facing aloneness," I said. Now she grew extremely interested. A therapist personal tool can look like a jewel to a patient desperate for answers.

"When I am confronted with those negative thoughts of not being part of my surroundings this is what I think: life has brought me where I am today because I need to learn something. Otherwise I would be somewhere else." Sabina looked at me but did not say a word. "You see," I went on, "the only way not to feel disconnected from life is to find a meaning to our experiences. Life's meaning has to do with learning how to unmask our own ghosts and you can only do that in solitude."

DIVORCE, THE REAL FRIEND TESTER

I remember a long time ago reading an article about the reactions people have to other people's divorce. The article had been written by a woman who had been divorced for a while, and although it presented many interesting ideas, what really stayed with me through the years was that for the author the worst part of divorcing someone had to do with other people's reactions. At that time it seemed surprising to me that a sad situation like a divorce would induce others to be unkind to fellow human beings. But when time passed and I had the opportunity to hear the same comment from several of my women patients, I began to analyze the reason behind this kind of attitude. One case especially comes to mind.

Alice was a 48 year old woman who had been married for more than 20 years. She had 2 sons and a daughter, all of them teenagers. Although the marriage had had some difficulties through the years, both Alice and her husband seemed determined to make it work. Or so it seemed for a while. Then things started to change. When she came to see me for the first time, Alice described her current situation as a nightmare.

"I can't believe this is happening to me, after all these years of being together."

As is the case in many modern marriages, Alice had discovered some compromising emails that her husband had sent to a co-worker. From the tone of the messages it was obvious that both had been carrying on an affair for a while. Alice was deeply distraught. The fact that her husband had lied to her for so many months had left her with a deep narcissistic wound that she found difficult to heal. Her self-esteem was shattered and she felt very vulnerable. Unfortunately things got even worse. Since she had decided to divorce from her husband, she started spreading the word among her friends. Although most of her friends and acquaintances were sincerely moved by her situation, others reacted with a total lack of compassion. Alice was flabbergasted. She had never expected this reaction from anybody she knew. I vividly remember one afternoon when she came to session in tears.

"Not only did I have to endure the sorrow of my husband's betrayal. Now the lack of compassion some people have shown towards me is beyond belief," she complained.

"Divorce," I explained to her, "can bring about very strange reactions from different people, especially those whose marriages are stagnant or beyond help, but who refuse to accept the reality of their own situation."

She mentioned the case of a woman, not really her friend but someone she had seen fairly regularly when she was married, whose comment had been something like "What a pity! Now the four of us will not be able to go out together anymore!" Or worse yet, a friend who had given her the following answer when she desperately asked her:

"Do you think there is anything I can do about this?"

"No, there is nothing you can do," had been her friend's short and abrupt answer. "It's over."

When Alice recalled this episode in session, I asked her to tell me more about this friend's life. Alice told me that her friend had been married for more than 25 years, that she had 2 teenage daughters and a husband who had been a fairly successful entrepreneur. However, with the economic downturn his luck had waned and he was now being supported by his wife's salary. Needless to say, his wife was not very happy with the situation. The fact that Alice's soon to be ex-husband had been a successful banker all his life had generated in many of her less fortunate friends feelings of envy. When the news spread about her divorce, those feelings of envy surfaced uncontrolled.

"What you need to remember," I told Alice, "is that we all talk about ourselves. Human beings can only comprehend their own reality, not other people's world. When your friend told you that there was nothing you could do about your marriage, she was really talking about her own wish of you not being able to fix your marriage. She has probably been envious of your economic well-being for many years and now she is enjoying a little feeling of revenge. She sees that you are vulnerable and in desperate need for company and she attacks you. But it's all about her own pain, not about you."

My explanation did not seem to convince my patient and the friendship eventually ended. Alice had taken personally her friend's abruptness and lack of understanding and had decided to look elsewhere for more compassionate companions.

GIVE UP TOMORROW

("The Untold Story of Paco Larrañaga and the Cebu's Trial of the Century", a documentary by M. Colins and M. Syjuco)

Give Up Tomorrow is the true story of Paco Larrañaga, a 19 year old man sentenced to death for the rape and murder of two sisters despite overwhelming evidence to the contrary. In the documentary, as he goes through his ordeal, Paco says to one of his interviewers that despite all that is happening in his life he will continue fighting for his freedom. He then adds: *"I will give up tomorrow."* When I saw the film I was horrified at the thought of someone having to face such a terrible karma. I also thought of Paco's mother who believed in him and fought incessantly to save his life. Finally the death penalty was abolished and Paco, a dual Filipino-Spanish citizen, was transferred to Spain to serve the rest of his sentence in that country. When released from jail Paco will be 61 years old and will have spent almost all his life incarcerated. When watching the film we cannot but think about the amazing inner strength of all people involved in this desperate situation, and their resolve to do whatever they can to save a life. However, without going to the extremes of situations like Paco's, it is undeniable that we all face difficult or very difficult situations in our lives where not giving up requires all the energy that we can muster. Such was the case of Adriana, a patient I had met for the first time many years ago. Adriana had come to see me when her two sons were teenagers. As a divorced mother it was difficult for her to handle a 16 and a 17 year old without a male role model in the home. Adriana was originally from a Central American country, and after her divorce she had moved to the United States while her sons' father stayed behind. I still remember how impressed I was by her beauty and her elegance the first time I saw her. Despite having being born in a very rich family, Adriana was very open and friendly and on more than one occasion, despite the severity of the issues discussed in session, we found a way to make a joke and share a laugh. Time went by and she stopped coming. Her sons were already grown and she had moved on with her life. It was many years later that I received a call from her on my way to work. We spoke briefly over the phone and agreed to meet for a session that same week. I was curious to hear how she was doing and I looked forward to seeing her again. After all, Adriana was one of those patients that therapists enjoy treating. When she finally came I could see right away that her life had not been a rose garden. Although she still looked attractive and was elegantly dressed, she seemed concerned and worried. We jumped right away into what had brought her to my office. In a few words I learned that Adriana had lost all her savings and that she was working as a massage therapist at a spa near my office. But that was not all.

"I am not happy with this job," she explained to me, "but it's a paycheck every two weeks. Now the owner has asked me to resign because she wants her niece to take my place. I have only one month's rent saved," she added. "That is all I have."

I looked at her in silence, trying to mentally devise a strategy that would help my patient start moving on. My utmost concern was to be realistic. I also wanted to sound convincing, but first I had to convince myself that there was a way to solve this dire situation in less than a month.

"Could you go live with your sister for a while until you find a new job?" I ventured.

"If I have no other option... But she lives in a tiny apartment and I could not stay with her for long."

After brainstorming several options I asked Adriana to bring me her resume next time so as to start planning where to file applications for work. I also suggested that she invest a little money in business cards to distribute in the neighborhood. She agreed and before leaving she said to me: "I know that I am protected." During the session I had sensed that Adriana was severely depressed and when she left I felt concerned. What gave me some peace of mind was the way she took leave of me: "*I know that I am protected*," had been her words. Before leaving my office Adriana had scheduled an appointment for the following Friday. However, two days after our first session she called me at my cellular.

"Do you believe in coincidences?" She asked anxiously. Her voice was breaking up.

"Coincidences don't exist," I said. "Everything is tied together and things follow a causal order."

"Well, let me tell you what happened to me yesterday. I can hardly believe it," she added overjoyed. "I went to get my paycheck at the spa and found no space to park my car. So I asked the receptionist at another spa located on the same block if I could leave my car in their parking lot for fifteen minutes. I explained to her that I had come to pick up my last paycheck and that it would only take me a short while. She asked me if I was leaving my job and I told her that I was and asked her to let me know if there was an opening at her spa. After picking up my check I came back to my car and found a note on the windshield: *Before you leave, please come inside. We are looking for a massage therapist because ours left.*

"Didn't I tell you I was protected?" Adriana almost screamed. "Had I found room to park my car in front of my spa I would have missed this job offer." I was speechless. Needless to say her therapy ended right there and then.

ALL IS LOST (The movie)

The other night I decided to watch a movie in Netflix that has to do with a man (Robert Redford) lost at sea who tries desperately to save his life after his damaged sailing boat has to face a violent storm. Since the boat radio and the navigation equipment are disabled, Redford will use all the resources at hand to try to overcome the many hurdles generated by the elements. What is most interesting is the fact that the movie has no dialogue so our attention as spectators is exclusively focused on how ingenious a human being can become when faced with a critical situation. The final scene of the movie is absolutely unforgettable: while Redford is finally giving up and ready to drown, he looks up towards the ocean surface and sees a boat hull and an extended hand in the water looking for survivors. When watching the movie I was almost hypnotized by looking at Redford digging up one resource after the other as the situation grew gradually worse. The fact of the matter is that he did not give up until the end when he realized that death was unavoidable; even then he still hesitated and gazed at the water surface one last time. After the movie ended I said to myself that we could perhaps draw a parallel with our own attitudes when confronted with life crises. Do we dig up new resources as we go along or do we give up in hopelessness and stop trying? Even in those situations where we can guess right away that all is lost, especially if it's a vital issue like a marriage, I believe it's important to exhaust all available options before calling it quits. That is, if we don't want to regret it in the future. Although the situation might seem hopeless, who knows? Something might come up out of the blue, like the hand in the movie, that will help us climb out of the abyss. Like Redford, Chiara's life had faced her with a critical situation. Her husband had told her that he wanted to start a new life without her. His decision took her by surprise, not because she wasn't aware that her marriage was not a happy one but because she considered her husband to be like a brother who would never desert the family. Chiara came from a traditional European family where, as she told me, grandparents, parents and siblings all fought with each other but nobody ever thought about leaving. On top of everything else Chiara's husband looked a lot like her brother, which made the projection even easier. On the other hand, Chiara's husband was raised in a totally different family, one in which nobody fought but where issues were swept under the rug. He was also raised by more liberal parents and he did not think twice once he had made up his mind to get a divorce. Needless to say, Chiara was devastated and did not know where to turn. So she came to see me with the hope that I could help her regain her emotional balance. The first thing I told her when she came to my office was that unfortunately bereavement is such that it takes time to heal. Loss is not overcome easily because if it were easy to be set aside it would not be our road towards wisdom. When it comes to emotional matters shortcuts are not effective. What I mean by shortcuts is that those of us who in order to forget someone start going out with whomever comes by, sooner or later will find out that that road leads to a dead end. It's better to pack a few things for the road and start walking. *A Journey of a thousand miles starts with a single step* (*). But that is not the only thing I told Chiara. I also told her that when we stop looking for easy answers, something will happen that will change our lives drastically. Chiara was a wonderful patient and when after a year she decided to put an end to therapy, I missed her. Time went by and I didn't hear from her for a while until one day she called me again. "Hello", I said not at all surprised. For some reason I was expecting her call.

"Hi there. I am calling you with good news. When can I come to see you?"

When Chiara came to my office that week she was a totally different person: she looked younger than her age, she was elegant as always but more casual, and her face was all smiles.

"Tell me all about it," I said.

"To be honest, when I stopped therapy I was still feeling hopeless about my future," said Chiara.

"I did not know what to do with the rest of my life. I remembered you telling me that no matter what happens we should not give up because we never know what the future has in store for us.
"True."
"Well, you were right." She smiled. "Life is unpredictable. It's true that no two stories are alike but mine is really amazing," said Chiara.
I couldn't wait for her to start talking.
"After I quit therapy I started going out left and right with my girlfriends. I felt lonely and I desperately wanted to find someone to replace my ex-husband. Needless to say, although I met several men, none of them were my type," Chiara explained.
"They were probably not for you."
"No, they were not," she agreed. "I kept looking for a partner non-stop until one day, on a Sunday morning when I was still in bed, I started feeling bored with the way I was living my life. So I decided that I would stay home more and go out less," she explained.
"I see."
"Yes, I needed to be home. "
"It makes a lot of sense."
"Until....," my patient smiled, "one day I was home by myself and somebody knocked on my door."
"Who was it?" I tried not to sound too curious.
"The neighbor who parks his car next to mine. He came to tell me that I had made a mistake and had parked my car in his space."
"I guess that the rest is history," I laughed.

"Exactly", answered Chiara. "We have been going out ever since."
Like in the movie, even when we think that everything is lost, there is always a hand waiting to help us. We just need to be patient, reflect, and trust the Universe.

* Chinese proverb

PAIN IS INEVITABLE, SUFFERING IS OPTIONAL.

K.C. THIESEN

The other day I was surfing the internet when I suddenly came across the above quote. It immediately attracted my attention because it wisely summarizes in just one line an entire philosophy of life. For those of us who have read and studied the Buddhist texts, this quote will certainly remind us of the Four Noble Truths:

The truth of dukkha (suffering, anxiety and lack of satisfaction)
The truth of the origin of dukkha
The truth of the cessation of dukkha
The truth of the path leading to the cessation of dukkha.

When the Buddha left his father's palace to see what was outside, what he encountered was the pain that we human beings suffer by becoming ill, by becoming old, and by dying. He also realized that since everything around us is in a constant state of flux and lacks substance, our lives are very unsatisfactory. These observations led the Buddha to start his journey in search of the origin of suffering and how suffering can be overcome. Although his father had tried to shield him from reality, as soon as he set a foot outside the palace, the Buddha realized that pain is woven into the fabric of life and thus unavoidable. Sooner or later all of us will be faced with loss, loneliness, illness and death. Arthur Schopenhauer came to the same conclusion when he said that we can never be happy because we are continually seeking satisfaction for our never ending desires. Some of us will have more tragic lives than others. However, in one way or another, all of us will have to find a way to deal with pain constructively. That is why the quote I mentioned at the beginning of this article seemed to me so significant. In just one line the author calls our attention to an important difference: although we all face pain at some point in our lives, we still have the option of either living with the suffering or finding a meaning to what happened to us that will allow us to move on. It all depends on our expectations and what we believe the purpose of our life to be. As for me, it was not long ago that I realized that we are not on this earth to be happy. If that would be our purpose the lives of all of us would be total failures. Life purpose is definitely not to be happy but to learn the lessons that we need to learn in order to evolve. If we look at our life under the lens of it being a place of learning, suddenly our reality becomes more understandable. The other fact that we have to keep in mind is that we are the ones who choose the lessons we came to learn. Let's not forget that nothing that happens in our lives happens without our participation. As a result, we are all responsible for how enlightened we become. We do have a guide however and that is our unconscious. Our unconscious is our link to the Divine. Several years ago I suffered a deep emotional loss. The world as I had known it since my childhood suddenly collapsed and precipitated me into a series of panic attacks as well as a severe depression. I was lucky enough to have a very caring son and several very good friends beside me, but despite all their nurturing life suddenly became like a ghost train ride for me. I remember at that time watching an Eckhart Tolle's video in YouTube in which he said that it was through our wounds that we opened up to the Universe. But although I understood perfectly well what he was talking about, emotionally I was not ready to own it. It was only several years later that I came to realize that the loss I had suffered had been necessary for me to learn very significant lessons: learning to be humble, learning to be alone, learning to be myself, and most of all learning to trust the Universe. If we learn to read the signals that are sent our way and we follow them, the cosmic consciousness will show us the way. I know that in the years to come I will have to face other losses. However, I am now much better equipped than in the past. Hopefully the serenity I have finally acquired will stay with me forever.

JUST START BY ASKING FOR FORGIVENESS AND THE REST WILL FLOW

The other day a good friend of mine asked me why I had decided two years ago to write a blog. Although in the beginning I thought I was writing a blog of patients' cases so that other people would benefit from the experience of fellow human beings, I gradually realized that I was mainly writing it for myself. At the time I started writing this blog my personal life was in disarray, so much so that every time I wrote a post I had to make sure not to include details of my personal life into my patients' cases. But since some of my patients' experiences were so similar to mine, they helped me better understand my own enigmas. As I mentioned in several of my posts, life is a place of learning. Every life situation that confronts us is a lesson to be learned in order for us to become better human beings. It is true that some lessons are more significant than others, but at the end of the day each one of our life experiences contains the wisdom that we need to become the person we need to become. There is however one life lesson that is so significant that I believe supersedes all others and that is to learn humility. In his classic Mussar text *The Duties of the Heart,* Rabbi Bahya ibn Paquda wrote that *"all virtues and duties are dependent on humility."* For those of us who have decided to embark on a spiritual path, our first step is to become humble. No easy task for sure. Fortunately for us, life itself will provide us with plenty of experiences that will help us start walking down the path of humility. Humility has to do with many things but especially with acknowledging the wrongs we do to others. Acknowledging what we did to others that caused them pain means to ask for their forgiveness so that we can cleanse our heart. If we don't do this, no matter how strongly we wish to leave the past behind and start again, we will never be able to do it successfully. Our entire life will become a vicious circle of mistakes and false starts and we will lose the opportunity of becoming more evolved human beings. Jose was one of those patients. He came to see me at a time when he had decided to divorce the mother of his children. As soon as he set foot in my office and started explaining to me why he was there, I could tell that his was a severe case of narcissistic personality disorder. The reason why he wanted a divorce was because of an event that had happened many years ago that he could never forgive nor forget. On one occasion his wife had gone to visit her family in her country of origin and while she was there Jose had had an episode of shingles. He called his wife to let her know but she did not offer to come back to take care of him. Jose had become incensed and from then on started concocting a plan for revenge. And so he did. In no time he had an affair with a work colleague and started living a double life. The therapy was very short lived because I could see that my patient had already made up his mind about his future. Although I tried my best I was unable to make him understand that if his wife had acted that way it was probably because he had done similar things to her in the past. Since Jose was not motivated to attend couple's therapy sessions, his long-term marriage broke up. However, after the breakup Jose's wife Elsa came to see me. What she had to tell me I had already guessed. During their years together Jose had been a very distant husband and not the companion she had hoped he would be when they married. Theirs had been the typical couple where one is the boss and the other tags along. In other words, the balance of power was tilted. Elsa was there to serve Jose and Jose was there to be served. That is why, when he came down with shingles, Elsa did not even think about coming back to be with him. As she explained to me, she had not done this to get back at him. Hers had been an unconscious decision. Only later did she realize that her decision had led her down the path of becoming herself. Time went by and Elsa called me for a new appointment. This time it was to tell me that Jose was getting married again. As she explained to me, Elsa was not sad because she wanted him back but because Jose's marriage marked the end of a dream.

"I cannot avoid realizing that his marriage underscores the loss of my life project," she said. "Being divorced does not mean that the family is broken. But with a new marriage, a stranger will enter my family circle."

"It's true," I said. "Your children will now have to deal with a different and more painful situation than if the two of you were divorced but had not remarried." I sighed before I went on. Elsa's story brought home some pain of my own.

"Let me ask you a question," I said. "Did you ever ask Jose for forgiveness for not having come back when he was sick?"

"I did," said Elsa. "I was able to put myself in his shoes and feel the pain he must have felt at the time, and I told him so."

"Did he ask you for forgiveness for the things he did to you?"

"No, he didn't."

"If he didn't then he hasn't learnt anything from this life experience and he is bound to repeat the same mistakes."

"What do you mean?" asked Elsa.

"What I mean is that life is repetitive. If we don't learn the right steps once, we will stay stuck. We can't go forward. In order not to fall in a vicious cycle of errors we have to acknowledge our mistakes and make amends. The first step towards transformation is asking others to forgive our wrongs. There is no way around it."

BLESS YOUR ENEMIES AND LET THEM GO...OR NOT?

There are events in our lives that leave forever a trace in our hearts, events that give us the impression that they will be present even in our deathbed. Some of these events might not be too significant; however, the pain they inflicted on us is still alive and well in our emotional memory. They are very much like a mental list of happenings which do not fade even with the passing of time. There they are, emanating some kind of negative energy in our lives. Our childhood is rich with these sad stories: sibling rivalries, fights with our best friends, the bullying, the teachers who did not like us, and so on and so forth. But these events did not happen only when we were young. A lot of them took place later in life; for example, if we were divorced and many of our acquaintances stopped calling or when some of our friends made painful remarks about our new life situation. When time goes by and we grow closer to the end rather than to the beginning of life we suddenly feel the urge to dot the i's and cross the t's with all those people who hurt us. Gabriela was a therapist. We had met a long time ago at a community mental health center where we worked with geriatric patients. Gabriela was in her mid-sixties, clever and thoughtful, and with a look of deep honesty in her eyes. She had found my phone number through a common colleague and she called me to schedule an appointment to brainstorm a very important decision she had to make. The day she came to my office I immediately recognized her. Although years had gone by, she was still the same affectionate person with whom I had shared so many work lunches.

"What brings you here?" I smiled. "It's not that often that a therapist comes to see me."

"I have an important decision to make and I need to brainstorm it with a therapist," was her answer. "But let me start from the beginning. Since long ago I have had in my mind a list of five or six people who hurt me for no reason. To be precise, people who projected on me their own lack of self-esteem. Actually, the list is longer but some of these people have already passed away," she said. "For many years I looked for their email addresses or their phones until I was able to find them. To ease my resentment I need to call them or write to them to let them know how I felt about them mistreating me. I think it's the only way to get them out of my system." Gabriela was silent for a moment while looking through the window of my office. I waited for her to continue and when she did she asked a question. "What do you think?" I waited a few seconds before answering. After all it was not an easy question.

"If you think that facing these people will be beneficial, go for it," I said. "As long as you do it well."

"What do you suggest? "

"I know that when we are angry it's more difficult to organize our thoughts and that our speech sounds nonsensical and disorganized." I said. "A brief message explaining why you are writing without offending or sounding that you are looking for vengeance should be OK."

"I am not looking for vengeance," Gabriela quickly answered. "I only need to let them know how much their attitude or their words hurt me. I will leave vengeance in life's hands," she added enigmatically.

That was the only session I had with Gabriela that year. But the following year she called me to schedule another appointment.

"How have you been?" I asked her when she came into my office with a self-assured demeanor. "Did you carry out your plan after all?"

"Yes, that's why I came back to see you," was her answer.

"Tell me."

"As you suggested, I wrote a brief script and I adapted it to every situation. Then I emailed it or called these people over the phone."

"Did they answer you?"

"Just one person emailed me back."

"To apologize?"

"No, to tell me that she did not remember the situation I was talking about," said Gabriela. "If they answered or not is not what matters." she added. "The most important thing is that I feel I pulled a load off my shoulders."

"Was this something you thought about often?" I asked.

"Yes. A couple of years ago I started putting my inner house in order." Gabriela explained. "I think we all reach an age in which we need to do this to start a new life stage. It has to do with closure. And although I did not feel pain for these past events any longer, I needed to face these people in some way. No matter how long ago it happened, I think it's a matter of self-respect and of setting our boundaries. We need to set a limit on what behaviors we are going to tolerate from others. After completing this task I felt that my boundaries were more secure. Now there are no more burdens from the past in my personal space and I can move towards my new life stage with more freedom."

PEOPLE WHO HURT US ARE HURTING

The above saying has always had a profound effect on me, not because I don't know that others can hurt us but because even our very good friends, when they are in pain, sometimes act or speak to us in hurtful ways. When we are in pain many times we are unaware of our surroundings because we focus entirely on ourselves. Feelings of desperation, sorrow, loneliness and resentment pervade us and our mind and our heart are out of our conscious control. One of the most common reactions is to throw our frustration at someone else as if by doing so we could get rid of it. Like the man who is reprimanded by his boss and goes home and kicks his dog. It is very unfortunate that in moments like these we lack the ability to think about the consequences of our actions. As a result of this lack of control often our relationships will change forever. That is why Elisa's story did not surprise me at all. I had been seeing Elisa for several months to provide her with post-divorce therapy. She was having a lot of difficulties getting over the disruption of her marriage, especially because she had dedicated many years of her life to the care of husband and children. When the children moved out of the house, the husband started becoming very distant and the rest is history. After her divorce Elisa started looking for a divorce group to attend until she found one at her neighborhood church. Although she did attend those sessions for several months she realized that she needed more individualized help. That is how she ended up in my office. Elisa did very well in therapy because she was one of those patients who are able to grasp the fact that a divorce is never a one person's move and that she too had participated in the marital breakup. Being a very analytically oriented patient, she was able to see how throughout the years she had started moving gradually towards her separation. Her husband, of course, had played the game with perfectly synchronized decision-making. When we are able to see what really lies behind an event we can leave behind our role of victims of circumstances and take control of our lives. However, her divorce had left Elisa with a sense of isolation that was generated by the loss of a significant attachment figure. As a result, an email or a phone call from her ex-husband always made her very happy. Then one day her birthday came along. As he always did, her ex-husband sent her a present. When she opened it Elisa was agreeably surprised to see it was an excellent perfume that had just hit the stores. But what made her feel really happy was that her ex-husband had chosen a perfume with a significant name:

J'adore (I adore in French.) For a moment Elisa was able to shed that daily feeling of loneliness and isolation that the divorce had brought into her life. For an instant she was able to dream that life could go back and be better, happier. That afternoon one of her friends called her to chat. Elisa was so happy with the present she had just received that she couldn't wait to tell her friend all about it. We women are lucky enough to be able to live our significant moments twice by sharing them with our friends. After telling her friend about the present, Elisa waited for her reaction. But what happened next was a deep disappointment to say the least.

"That perfume was probably the least expensive in the store or it was on sale," her friend said. Needless to say, Elisa was speechless. At our next session we spent the whole hour analyzing the matter thoroughly.

"I could not believe my ears," said Elisa. "She is one of my very good friends," she added.

"Is she married?" I asked.

"Yes, although not to the best guy in the world."

"Does she get any gifts from her husband?"

"I am not sure'" she answered. "I remember that once we had gone out to dinner and she was wearing a very beautiful ring. I asked her about it and she told me that she had bought it herself during one of her trips" said Elisa with a pinch of satisfaction in her voice.

"There you go," I answered smiling.

"You are right," she said, smiling too. "When I was married I remember I once told my then husband not to bring me any more accessories because I already had more than I could wear, "she added.
"See?"
"Yes, but my friend doesn't know that," retorted Elisa. "All she knows is that now I am alone. How can she be so insensitive?"
"She is not being insensitive," I explained. "She is a woman in pain. The fact that your ex-husband gave you a nice present for your birthday perhaps reminded her that her husband totally forgets hers. And she doesn't even have the freedom to share her frustration with you. Hurting you eases her pain."

Middle Age: Our Road to Inner Wisdom

"...of his initiation into a new unknown life..."

Crime and Punishment.

F. Dostoyevsky

When Nancy came to see me at my office one beautiful spring afternoon, she had been divorced from her husband for seven years. From what she told me that day, those had been harrowing years in which only her pride had prevented her from falling apart completely. Nancy was a school counselor who had been married for more than 25 years to a very successful developer. They had married young and together had had a daughter. Although in the beginning the marriage had worked fairly well, as is often the case wealth and reputation had generated more than one problem in their relationship. In the beginning Nancy had not felt too concerned because she knew that every marriage has its ups and downs and hers was no different. But as time went by and her husband became more and more indifferent, her anxiety and fears started to grow. That is when she called me to make an appointment. People usually come to see me with one goal in mind: solve the problem at hand. When we feel desperate it is very difficult to see the big picture. All we know is that we are hurting and that we need to ease the pain. As a therapist I have to meet my patients where they are at. So I listened attentively to Nancy's story and agreed that her situation was a critical one. As a general rule, when a patient comes alone to therapy and states that the partner is becoming distant, the first thing that comes to mind is that there is somebody else in the picture. This is of course critical information for patient and therapist because if the extramarital relationship is a serious one, then the marriage is in jeopardy. Unfortunately this was the case with Nancy's husband, so much so that he even refused to come to therapy for a session of closure. Time went by and Nancy kept coming to therapy. Together we went through the ending of her marriage with all the emotional and financial turmoil it entails, as well as the endless explanations due to daughter and friends. From the outside, Nancy could be thought of as a strong person going through a very difficult time with dignity and self-respect. However, deep down she couldn't even begin to grasp why this traumatic event had happened to her in the first place. After processing her grief for innumerable sessions, finally Nancy started to move on. Despite feeling a deep sense of loss, she had accepted the fact that her husband was not the man she had fell in love with. However, she was still struggling to find a meaning to this sad life experience. But one day she came to session looking more serene and I could sense that she had had a breakthrough. Nancy told me that she had just finished reading *Crime and Punishment* and that she wanted to discuss with me the novel's last page. Dostoyevsky ends this work by saying that Raskolnikov's stay in Siberia was necessary for him to pass into another world.

"Do you think that pain is the only way into a deeper life meaning and that is why we all have to suffer for one reason or another?" asked Nancy with some apprehension.

"I don't believe that pain alone will make us better people," I said. "What I believe is that all these painful experiences hide a lesson to be learned. While some people are able to learn and evolve, others unfortunately are not," I added.

"In the case of Raskolnikov, what would be the lesson to be learned?" Nancy went on.

'I believe that Raskolnikov stepped into the other world so to speak when he was able to accept Sofya's love for him and with the help of that love feel remorse for what he had done." I ventured. "While he was the prisoner of his own rationalizations for the murder committed, there was no way out of his private hell," I added.

"And what should I learn from my experience?" Nancy asked again. I smiled.

"Only you know the way into your other world," I said. "The only thing I can tell you is that a starting point is to become more humble and make amends with those you have hurt."

IF YOU DON'T KNOW THE ANSWER

ASK YOUR DREAMS

As I have stated many times in my blog, the idea of an almighty God that rules heaven and earth has become difficult for me to understand and accept. On the other hand, a universe without Divine energy also fails to convince me because in many occasions I have faced difficult life situations that I couldn't have solved without some kind of metaphysical intervention. I am sure this has happened to all of us, except that some of us still have difficulties seeing beyond physical reality, especially regarding all those events that have to do with our unconscious. I remember a very long time ago, when I was still in my student years, I had gone to see a therapist at the university counseling center. I had just come to live in the United States and universities in my native Argentina were like night and day as compared to the colleges in America. Although I spoke English I was not trained in making presentations in front of my fellow students, especially in a foreign language. Since I was afraid that my level of anxiety would get in the way of my studies, I went to see a university counselor to ask how to relax and overcome this phobia. I don't remember exactly what the counselor said except one thing: "Buy a notebook and write down all your dreams. In time you will find the answer." At that moment I remember thinking how lucky I was not to have to pay for such an enigmatic session. But since my performance anxiety was still alive and well, I followed the counselor's advice and bought myself a notebook. Every morning as soon as I woke up I wrote what I had dreamed the night before so as not to forget any of the details. Later in the day I would read what I had written and tried to interpret its meaning and its relation to what I was going through. One of the things that I remembered from the few counseling sessions I had attended was that my difficulty in presenting had probably to do with my being an introvert. According to Hans Eysenck introversion and extroversion have a biological basis: while introverts have a high cortical arousal and become overwhelmed in a crowd, extroverts on the contrary seek highly stimulating situations. However, despite this biological handicap I knew I had to overcome my avoidance and present. On the night before I had to do my first presentation I went to bed early and extremely nervous. I knew that if I wanted to pursue a career I had no option but to overcome my performance anxiety. After much turning around in bed I finally fell asleep and had the following dream: *I was in a garden with a man who was playing ball. At the end of the yard, next to a wall, there stood a plant with two branches. Although both branches were in bloom, one was taller and bigger than the other. I told the man to be careful with the ball so as not to break the plant. Two seconds after having said that the man kicked the ball and broke the taller branch. I looked at the plant in dismay and said to myself that the branch would die. Then I started to look in my dream at the smaller branch. Although more fragile it was also in bloom. I thought that although the bigger branch would surely die, the smaller branch would continue growing and become as tall as the other one.* The next morning I woke up refreshed and feeling lighter. At that point I still had not established a correlation between the dream and my performance anxiety, but I felt more confident and secure about presenting that afternoon. Needless to say, the presentation went well and I passed the course. But more important, although I did not know it at the time, that was the day when the second branch started to grow.

I DON'T HAVE TO CROSS AN OCEAN

TO FORGET YOU

I remember that in the romantic literature I use to read when I was young —nowadays I am reticent to read fiction simply because reality is more fascinating to me— the characters that were heartbroken went off on very long journeys across the world in the hope that geographic distance would help them forget their loved one. However, they were almost never able to put their losses behind them because, they concluded, losses lay deep down their hearts. As time went by (and many psychology books later) my view of the world changed. I started to understand how certain behaviors, even though they might seem superficial, can help us turn the pages of our life. When Solange came to my office she had been separated from her husband for four years. After almost twenty years of living together with their two children, both decided to call it quits. With that goal in mind they sold the family house and bought two apartments, not far from each other. In her own words, Solange's marriage had been based on a deeply loving partnership, but with time life difficulties started mining the relationship and a separation became inevitable. In all long term marriages, good or bad, separation is a very long process. It usually starts long before the actual separation takes place. In Solange's case both partners ended up buying apartments close to each other probably because, even though they were not living together any longer, they were still emotionally close. In the beginning of her separation Solange felt comforted to have her ex-husband near her. Even though they only saw each other at family gatherings, having him physically close made her feel protected. However as time went by the fact of merely seeing him walk by her house made her feel a deep longing for the life they had shared. Although several years had already passed since her separation and divorce, Solange realized that she still had not turned the page of her marriage and that it was time for her to do something about it. She thought that perhaps having a session of closure with her ex-husband could help her end the relationship once and for all. That was when she came to see me, referred by a friend who had been a patient of mine. After explaining the reason of her call, I asked her what was her specific goal in having this last session with her ex-husband. It was then that she told me that during the last four years she had started thinking of the many misunderstandings that had taken place between her ex-spouse and herself, and that she felt the need to clarify certain things and, if necessary, make amends. While Solange was talking I realized that she still had not been able to overcome the loss of her marriage and that the session of closure was merely an excuse to have a new encounter with her ex-husband. However, I decided not to mention this to her and backed her up with her plan because a session of closure to clarify past misunderstandings is always significant and useful. Our strategy was to have Solange wait a few days to make sure that she really wanted to go ahead with her plan, and if so she would call her ex-husband and invite him to a conjoint session. After a couple of weeks Solange called me to schedule a new appointment. When I asked her if she was planning to come with her ex-spouse, she said that she wouldn't and that she would explain to me why during our session. Once in my office I asked her what had happened. The answer was that as we had agreed she had called her ex-husband to invite him to a conjoint session but that he had declined.

"Did he give you any reasons of why he didn't want to come?" I asked.

"Yes. He said that we had already talked about all the things we needed to talk about and that it made no sense to talk once more about the past," was her answer.

That was the last time I saw Solange that year. Time went by and I totally forgot about her until one day, two years later, I received a call from her wanting to schedule an appointment. When I saw her come into my office on that summer day I realized immediately that her life had significantly changed for the better. Not only had she lost some weight and was more neatly dressed, but also her gait was more dynamic and she looked happier.

"You look great" I complimented her.

"I finally started living again," she said without blinking. "Today I came for a session of closure, but with myself", she laughed.

"How so?" I wanted to know.

"After my ex-husband declined my invite to come to a final session, I realized that I had no other option but to put an end to that stage of my life on my own. That is when I realized that some geographical distance between us might be helpful.

"Are you thinking of moving to another state?" I asked her with surprise.

"No. I want to move to another neighborhood", she said.

I waited for her to elaborate.

"The apartment in which I now live is the apartment of loneliness and despair. It's the apartment I bought after my separation, and although it's a beautiful place it exudes pain and remembrance." Solange was silent for a moment as if waiting for my reaction to her words. I chose not to interrupt her line of thought. She went on.

"Even though I will continue living in the same city as my ex-husband, I feel that moving to a new neighborhood and to a new house will be the real end of my marriage and the start of a new day".

"I agree," I said. "You don't need to cross an ocean to put some physical distance between the two of you. A new house will provide you with renewed energy."

"Yes, and although my memories, my happy moments and my regrets will always be with me, my new home will not be a place to lick my wounds but a place to start anew."

*PEACE OF MIND HAS NOTHING TO DO
WITH US WISHING EVENTS TO BE WHAT
WE WANT THEM TO BE BUT WITH
ACCEPTING THEM AS THEY ARE.*

EPICTETUS

Since this idea is linked to prayers and religious tenets (*Thy will be done on earth as it is in heaven*) I had never paid too much attention to its meaning. I am spiritual but not religious. The idea of a creator does not convince me and I am still struggling to devise a coherent view of the universe. However, the more books I read that have to do with the meaning of life, the more convinced I become that all that happens to us, good or bad, is part of a plan. We often find in Eastern philosophy the metaphor of life as a tapestry where all the threads are needed to form the design. The interesting thing however is that life tapestry is being woven as we go along so that its final design can only be seen the last day of our lives. What this means is that it is only then that we will understand the plot. A Buddhist would argue that the bad things that happen to us are the result of our karma from past lives. Decisions we made in the past, in this life or in the life that came before this one, have consequences that have ripened in our current circumstances. These consequences are none other, Buddhists state, than the unhappy events in our lives. This Buddhist paradigm makes sense to me. More than once I have seen people pay for the pain they have inflicted unto others. I have seen this happen so many times that I sometimes have asked myself if it's not our unconscious the one to induce us to be punished in order to be cleansed. Criminals have been known to make a mistake and dial 911 instead of the number they needed to dial. When they realized their mistake a police car had already been dispatched to their location. Whatever the situation, peace of mind has to do with accepting the fact that the "bad things" that happen to us need to happen and are none other than learning experiences in our path towards self-realization. I agree with Christopher Vogler in his foreword to *Myths and the Movies* by Stuart Voytilla when he states that the hero's journey starts with a central dramatic question that disrupts his/her ordinary life. Ordinary life is the hero's comfort zone that is being challenged by a dramatic event. At this point the hero –all of us—can either try to understand the meaning of the challenge, or go against the flow of life and drive him/herself to despair. Accepting the challenge means to be willing to sail into uncharted waters. If we refuse to face the challenge at hand, it will come back to haunt us at a later date. However, when we start navigating into the unknown we will probably find the directions we need. Life's goal is not fame, wealth, or daily contentedness but self-knowledge. If we came to this difficult world it's because we need to improve our knowledge of the Self. Most of all we need to conquer fear. Sergio was referred to me by one of my longtime patients. He was a very friendly 40 years old, married with 5 children. He had come to the United States from Chile where his very large and traditional family of origin resided. When he told me that his family was very close-knit and well-off, I asked him why he had decided to leave his country to come to the United States. His answer was that a friend of his had offered him a good position in his real estate business. Although his explanation did not convince me, I took it at face value for the time being. Sergio was having severe marital issues. I had met his wife in our family sessions and since the beginning I realized that it was going to be very difficult to mend the relationship. Not so much because of Sergio —as a matter of fact he was extremely motivated to make his marriage work- but because his wife displayed a severe narcissistic personality disorder that made marital therapy almost impossible. When his wife decided not to attend marital sessions any longer, Sergio kept coming to session with the hope of finding a way to save his marriage. The only idea of divorcing and having to live without his children upset him in such a way that it took him almost three years to understand that a separation was inevitable. The months that followed his decision to finally move out of the house were very difficult for him.

"I remember you telling me when I first met you that you thought it was better to repair a marriage than to divorce, especially when there are children involved," he told me once while in session and in the midst of a deep emotional turmoil.

"I still believe what I said," was my answer. "But in order to repair a marriage we need two people with enough motivation to do it. In your case we only have one person who is willing to honestly look at himself and change what needs to be changed."

As time went by Sergio became less depressed and more able to realize that his divorce from his wife had been inevitable. He invested a lot of his energy in his work, rented a nice apartment and invited his children often to dinner. Gradually he even started enjoying his evenings at home alone. Nowadays we meet sporadically when a crisis arises, but Sergio is not the Sergio I met several years ago. Not only has he shed his dependent personality traits, but he can also set firm boundaries about what he will or will not tolerate from others. When we talk about his life in the last years we both agree that his journey towards self-realization started a long time ago, when he left his country of origin. Sergio remembers the many power struggles he had with his older brother and his mother and how he was always unable to stand up for himself. Now, when he travels to see them, he does not hesitate to set with them the same boundaries he was able to set with his now former wife. Even his demeanor has changed. Whereas before he walked as if carrying a heavy weight on his shoulders, he now looks at the world from a strong angle. The painful events that happened in Sergio's life –and in all our lives- needed to happen for him to become the person he is now. Understanding this fact gives him the peace of mind he needs to move on and look at his future with optimism

BEWARE OF PARENTAL MANDATES

We are usually unaware of how powerful our family of origin tenets are. Because they are often subliminal, these messages have been embedded in our minds slowly but surely while we were living under our parents' roof. Usually these tenets are part of our family history, a history that our parents have inherited from their own parents when they were children. When we grow up, these messages exert a powerful influence on our lives by sometimes making us make decisions that are not always beneficial to us. Carlos is a good example of how these messages can disrupt our adult relationships and even generate sickness and depression in our lives. He was referred to me by his sister, who had been my patient a long time ago. Carlos was a handsome 55 year old professional man, who came to see me because he had just divorced his wife of 28 years. Although he was Jewish, Carlos had an interfaith marriage with a Catholic woman. Since nor Carlos or his wife were religious when they were married, religion did not play any role in their life at that time. Not so in Carlos's family however. Although Carlos' mother was not very religious, she had always hoped that her son would marry a Jewish woman. She had never been that explicit but she often said that if a Jew married a gentile, when they argued the gentile would tend to call the Jew names. Carlos had never paid attention to his mother's words (or so he thought) but when his sons were born, Carlos started paying more attention to Jewish traditions. As a result he told his wife that for him it was very important that his sons be brought up Jewish. His wife readily accepted because not only was she not religious, but she also had deeply anticlerical ideas —also a consequence of her childhood-. As time went by and their oldest son approached his bar mitzvah age, Carlos asked his wife to take his son every Sunday to the temple for his religious education. Since his wife was the boys' main caretaker she considered this as one of her motherly duties and started taking her son to Sunday school for his bar mitzvah preparation. All went well and after the ceremony Carlos profusely thanked his wife for being so generous. Theirs was a good marriage and the wife's gesture had definitely made them even more involved with each other. However, seasons came and went and as it's usually the case, when the youngest son left home to attend college, conflicts and marital dissatisfactions started to simmer. Carlos and his wife had no choice but to face the fact that in their marriage there were many hidden conflicts at work that had been swept under the rug. Since his wife had been in charge of the home logistics, Carlos was able to focus almost entirely on his work. As a result, after years of working hard he had become a very successful professional and when his youngest son left for college he started spending more time at work than at home. The obvious consequence of this was an affair with a younger colleague. During those years, on the rare moments that Carlos was at home he was not the nicest guy to be around. It was not long before his wife started realizing that something in her marriage was awfully wrong. Because she was so concerned and scared, she started nagging Carlos in such a way that the relationship became unbearable. Carlos tried to hide his extramarital relationship in the best way possible until one day his unconscious (as it usually happens) played him a dirty trick. He left on a trip "forgetting" that his wife had his computer password and leaving in Outlook all his lover's emails. When he came back all hell broke loose and both he and his wife decided to separate. Two years later they made their separation final through a divorce. At the time of his divorce Carlos fell ill with bronchitis and severe asthma attacks. Interpreting his illness as a psychosomatic symptom of their divorce and seeing that her ex-husband was not doing well, Carlos' wife thought reconciliation would be possible. But although he kept in touch with his ex-wife fairly often, for Carlos their separation was for good.

"Why were you so convinced that a reconciliation was impossible?" I had asked him when he came to see me complaining of a post-divorce depression.

"Because I knew that my wife would never forgive me and living together would be impossible" had been his answer. Although he acknowledged that he loved his wife and that she was a wonderful person, he did not see it as a possibility for them to start their relationship anew. However, when Carlos gave me more details about his family of origin, I immediately suspected that something deeper was at play in his reluctance to give his marriage another chance. Time went by and Carlos started becoming more interested in Jewish religion, going to the temple for the annual Jewish celebrations and socializing with other members of the congregation. One day the rabbi introduced Carlos to a Jewish woman ten years his junior. They soon started having a relationship and, as he then told me in one of our sessions, Carlos felt life had given him another chance at love. Because the relationship is still ongoing we will not be able to assess if Carlos' choice of leaving a good marriage was a good idea.* However, the fact that his new partner is Jewish makes me wonder if all his actions since day one were not related to his unconscious need to abide by his mother's mandate. It's amazing how many detours we will take in our lives to comply with our parents' wishes. The only way of rebelling against these mandates is by understanding that we came to life to achieve our own self-realization and not comply with our parent's wishes. Only through a healthy individuation from our family of origin can we live an authentic life.

- As this book was being published, Carlos' second marriage was already starting to fall apart.

THERE IS A TIME FOR EVERYTHING

(ECCLESIASTES 3:1.8)

When Adriana called me to make an appointment, hers was a different kind of appointment than the one that usually brings patients to my office. As a matter of fact she stated that she was not interested in starting any kind of treatment. She just needed a one time consultation. I told her that it would be up to her to decide how to use her time in session. This said we scheduled an appointment for the following week. When she came to my office, Adriana's calm demeanor told me right away that she had reached this stage in her life with serenity. Adriana was a middle age woman, still attractive, but with that beauty that has more to do with inner knowledge than with physical traits. Minutes after we started the session, Adriana told me that she was a professional with several years of experience in her field, that she was lucky enough to hold a good job, that she had a successful grown daughter as well as a nice group of women friends. She had been living alone for quite some time. As she spoke I had the time to observe her demeanor. Her tone of voice was calm and self-assured, and she had all the appearance of having more answers than questions.

"What brings you to my office?" I asked her with curiosity. "You said you wanted to consult with me about an issue."

"That's right", she answered. "I have been thinking about consulting a therapist on a topic that has been bothering me for a while now."

"What is it," I said inviting her to start talking.

"For some time my friends and I have been wondering about the following question: is it necessary in middle age to have a partner in order to be happy? Some of my friends are convinced that alone they will never feel completely satisfied, while others feel that the time to have a partner is gone and that it is better to live middle age in a different way."

"And what do you think?" I asked her although I already knew what would be her answer.

"I believe that at my age it is very difficult to have a relationship that works. All of us come to this life stage with a baggage too heavy to share with another human being", she concluded.

While listening to her I could not avoid smiling. How many times my friends and I had approached the same subject without ever agreeing? My smile prompted Adriana to ask me why I was smiling.

"It has nothing to do with you," I explained. "I am smiling because it's a subject that is present in my life too." It's not too often that I self-disclose with my patients. But when I feel that the information is relevant and that the patient can benefit from it, I do it without hesitation. Adriana looked at me in awe.

"In your life?"

"Yes, I said. "I have thought about it often. But what is important is not the conclusion I may have reached but the conclusion that is satisfactory to you", I added promptly.

"I can't reach any conclusion because although I feel OK with my life, when I see couples my age walking hand in hand I start to ponder."

"What do you ponder upon?"

"I start feeling scared that if I don't look for a partner now, then it will be too late and I will regret it."

"Do you feel lonely when you are alone at home?" was my question.

"Sometimes, but if that happens I call a friend and make plans to go out."

"Do you make plans every day or do you also stay home reading a book or watching a movie?"

"Some years ago I was unable to stay home alone," said Adriana." But now I enjoy it. Moreover", she added "when I am at home reading a book or watching a movie past dinner time I feel glad not to have to interrupt what I am doing to fix dinner for someone else."

"It's true that being in a relationship makes life more colorful," I answered." But it's also true that a relationship cannot always be peaceful and that sooner or later conflict will arise. There is no relationship without conflict. Perhaps you are thinking that, despite being alone, your peace and quiet are more valuable than having to deal with the daily demands of a relationship."

"Yes," she agreed. "The daily interactions of a relationship scare me to death. I have already lived it and I don't think that at this stage of my life I have the energy to relive it."

"Perhaps the reason is that every stage of life has a different purpose," was my comment. "When we are young our priority is finding a mate and having children, but in middle age our priority is acquiring knowledge.

"Knowledge?" asked Adriana?

"Yes, perhaps our purpose at this age is to learn, to reflect and to achieve self-realization." I ventured. "Since our responsibilities are fewer and we have more free time in our hands, we can finally immerse ourselves in pondering upon our existential questions. Remember that saying from the Ecclesiastes *there is a time for everything*"? Perhaps now is the time for you to reflect and search for a view of the universe that will give meaning to your life."

AM I OK WITH MY LIFE?

Florence had been a patient of mine when she was in her fifties. At that time she came to see me because her husband of 28 years had passed away after a long illness. Hers had been a good marriage, a relationship characterized by respect and equality. As a result, the passing of her husband had left Florence with a deep sense of loneliness and isolation. A friend had given her my name and she came to see me hoping that I would show her how to start living in the world as a single person again. As those of us who have travelled that path know, starting a social life as a single person after having being married for many years is far from easy. A friend of mine who became a widow at age 55 used to tell me that living alone came with the job of keeping in touch with almost everybody every day. Having a good social life can be a hard job indeed, especially for women. While single men no matter what age are usually invited to all sorts of events by the hostesses, single women are usually shunned sometimes even by their own friends, especially at middle age when marriages are so vulnerable. Fortunately, Florence had been able to overcome that hurdle. Thanks to her strong motivation not to let depression engulf her she had managed to meet several new friends. By participating in several book clubs and by going to concerts and workshops she had been able to make a new life for herself. That's why her phone call requesting an appointment took me by surprise. I wondered what was bringing her to my office once again. She came to see me one afternoon in the middle of summer. Although several years had passed, my former patient still looked energetic and well settled in life.

"What brings you here after all these years," I asked her with curiosity. "The last time I saw you, you were about to leave on a trip with some friends."

"Yes, I remember," she answered promptly. That was five years ago. That was a great trip." Florence stood silent for a while as if struggling about how to put into words the concern that had brought her to me. I also stood silent and waited for her to start talking.

"It's amazing that you mentioned that trip because the reason for my coming today is exactly that: I am having issues with some of my friends."

"Tell me all about it," I encouraged her.

"I am sure you remember that when my husband passed away I had to start meeting new people and getting myself a new life." she started saying. "

"Of course I remember," I answered.

"Well, I have to say that with the help of therapy I was able to pull myself together. After a year or two of becoming a widow I managed to build a very satisfying social life for myself." There was a silence again." But now things are changing a little."

"What do you mean?" I asked.

"Well, as years go by some of my friends are becoming grouchy and not very pleasant to be around," she explained. "In the beginning I said to myself that people are not perfect and that if I have a hard time tolerating others I will end up alone. But unfortunately some of these friends have changed a lot." At this point Florence looked at me inquisitively. "Why is life always so full of challenges? It's one hurdle after the other...Am I ever going to be able to rest?" Her tone of voice revealed her state of mind.

"I hear you Florence," I said. "But let me reframe your question. Let's ask ourselves why we people make life so difficult." I looked at her trying to guess if she agreed with me. She did.

"You are right," she said. "My question needed reframing."

"I am glad you agree with me on this," I said. "Now let me talk to you about Erik Erikson, who described life as a series of stages we go through. Does his name sound familiar?" I asked. Florence shook her head so I went on. "To be precise, Erikson talked about eight life stages. At each of these stages there is a psychological skill to be learned. If the learning does not occur when it should, we will be emotionally stuck until we master that skill. The first of these stages, the most important, occurs from birth to two years of age. The skill we acquire at this stage is trust. If we are born into an environment that does not facilitate this learning, then we will become mistrustful and trust will need to be learned later in life. On the other hand, the last stage occurs at 65 years of age. At that age our emotional skills should have been acquired and hopefully we can look at how we have lived our life with few regrets. If so we will be able to enjoy what is left to live and even face our death with serenity. However, if our life was marred by bad choices that we have no time to correct, then in our last years we will dwell in despair. Those are the friends that you are having difficulties with: they are depressed, irritable, and contemptuous."

Florence looked at me as if I had just revealed to her one of life's biggest mysteries. And perhaps I had revealed something very important to her: namely, that unlike some of her friends, she was able to enjoy her golden years because she had lived her life wisely.

"I DON'T NEED TO BELIEVE, I KNOW"

(C. JUNG, interview before his death)

Although it's true that most people come to my office to solve their daily struggles with life, once on a while it will happen that somebody will come to see me to discuss more metaphysical matters. Since at this stage of my life I am also struggling with my view of life after death, this type of sessions are extremely challenging and I have to be very cautious not to let my beliefs get in the way. Many times patients have started their spiritual quest with a difficult situation that was resolved and that left them wondering if this was an event like any other event in their lives —just luckier—or if it symbolized another dimension of reality. One of these patients —I will call her Carla—was one of those patients who had been trying for some time to find a satisfying answer to her spiritual questions. Her quest had started long ago, when she was 25 years old. At that time she lived with her parents in Argentina, and she was about to graduate with a degree in literature from the university of Buenos Aires. One summer weekend her parents decided to spend some time at a house they had built at a vacation resort near the city. Carla stayed behind, not only because she was preparing her thesis but because she had made plans with friends to go to the movies a have dinner afterwards. She came home at around 12am and went straight to bed. Suddenly she awoke to a very loud noise coming from the apartment's landing. The building where Carla's parents lived was a fairly old building with only two apartments per floor. Carla's apartment was located on the 4th floor and had the letter B while her neighbor's across the hall had the letter A. At first Carla thought that somebody had slammed a door and that the noise would end. But when the noise went on and she started hearing many people talking at the same time, some of them screaming, she got out of bed and went to check what was going on. When she came near the apartment door somebody started knocking really loud and screamed: "Open the door! Open the door." At this point Carla was panic stricken and barely able to move. The only thing she was able to realize was that these were not thieves. It had to be something else. So mustering up her courage she answered: "I am alone in the house and I am afraid. I need to call the police." Having said that she started dialing 911. The phone was near the entrance so whoever was knocking on the door could hear her conversation. When she started talking on the phone there was a silence. "I am home alone and some people are knocking at my door and want to come in," she said to the person who answered the 911 call. "What should I do?"

The answer was: "From the window can you see police cars on the street?"

Carla walked to the window to check.

"Yes."

"Then open the door." Carla felt more helpless than before the call. She understood that she had no options. She had to open the door or the people outside would break in. But as she was grabbing the doorknob she heard the voice of one of her neighbor's sons, who had just come back home, say: "Ms. X, I am here with a group of people in uniform who tell me they need to talk to you. Please open the door." As soon as Carla opened the door, as many as 7 or 8 military policemen rushed inside the apartment armed to their teeth. There was only one civilian man in the group. He stayed in the living room with Carla and her neighbor while his subordinates searched the whole apartment. The raid lasted for about 30' and after some questioning by the man in street clothes, they all left. Carla thanked her neighbor for his help and went back to bed. She was so shaken that she was unable to sleep for several days after that. One week after this incident, a group of military policemen raided the apartment 3B and kidnapped the owner's daughter. She was never to be found again. Her name was added to the very long list of young Argentines who "disappeared" during the military dictatorship.

"Tell me in what way this story was the starting point of your quest for a spiritual meaning of life" I asked my patient.

"Although there have been other instances in my life of events that pointed to the direction of a supra-reality," she started saying, "this story is extraordinary in one very specific way: the fact that my neighbor's son arrived home exactly at the moment when the police were knocking at my door. He later told me that when he opened the elevator's door he was asked who lived in apartment 4B. When he told them my father's name and last name they probably realized that they had come to the wrong place. But they wanted to make sure. So that is why when he asked me to open the door he used my last name. The person they were really looking for was living at 3B. But if my neighbor had not appeared at the scene exactly on time to tell them my name, they would have taken me away."

I was so moved by Carla's story that I couldn't say a word. All I could do was remember Jung's words when asked if he was a believer. "That is a difficult question to answer," he said smiling. "I don't need to believe...I know."

OUR UNCONSCIOUS, OUR TEACHER

According to Gnostic philosophers, self-knowledge is the knowledge of God. For Socrates an unexamined life is not worth living, and for Jesus in the Dialogue of the Saviors (Gnostic Gospels): "The lamp of the body is the mind." The most significant content of our mind is unconscious and our most significant life task is to make our unconscious conscious. Jung said: "What we don't know about our unconscious will become our fate." Fortunately, we are not alone in this task. Dreams are the messengers of our unconscious. When we are ready to learn a new step in our journey towards self-realization, our unconscious will send us a dream with all the elements we need to better understand a situation. Then we will only need to take notes and decode its symbolism. Decoding our dreams paves our way towards becoming the masters of our lives. Sarah had been struggling with a divorce for five long years. Like many other middle aged men, Sarah's husband had decided to leave the marriage once their daughter left for college. Needless to say Sarah was devastated and for many years had been unable to understand what had broken a family that she knew was not perfect but was sound and solid. In order to get help she started looking for a therapist and following the advice of a friend she called a Jungian therapist to make an appointment. Although still very depressed and with very little energy to even talk about her loss, Sarah complied with the appointment. When she arrived to the therapist's office, Sarah realized that she had come to the right place. Not only the therapist seemed to be a very compassionate person, but she was also a seasoned clinician who was able to transmit to her the hope in a better future. At that point, Sarah's journey towards self-discovery started. Several months went by and finally one day Sarah went to her appointment in a much better mood that in the past. When her therapist asked her what had changed, Sarah said that she had had a dream which she did not remember but that she had woken up the next morning with a deep sense of happiness and relief. Although she did not understand what had happened to her, Sarah said that since that day on she recovered her ability to enjoy the small things in life: reading a good book, going to the beach, sharing a drink with friends... Sometime after having that dream, Sarah ended treatment. After a couple of months she called me to make an appointment because, she said, she wanted to try another therapy orientation. After filling me in with what had happened in the last five years, she told me that lately she had been having a problem with one of her friends. This friend was a controlling and demeaning person, and the only reason why her friends kept seeing her was because they had known her for many years. The issues Sarah had been having with this particular friend had to do with her personality traits, traits that at this stage of her life Sarah could no longer tolerate. She had already tolerated for many years a husband with a severe narcissistic personality, who used to control and demean her every time the occasion arose. Now, after several years of therapy, Sarah could not accept her friend's lack of boundaries. But what really upset her was that after an argument she had had with her friend the week before she had lost her cool and again started feeling depressed. Sarah was afraid to undo all the progress she had made in therapy.

"Instead of helping me overcome my loss, all she does is rehash past events that can no longer be changed. She reminds me a lot of my ex-husband who did not miss any opportunity to demean me."

I told Sarah that analyzing her friend's behavior would be a waste of time and that we would make a much better use of our sessions if we concentrated on her feelings and intuitions.

"Did you have any dreams lately?" I asked so as to redirect her attention to her unconscious information.

"As a matter of fact I did," she answered surprised at not having thought of that before. "The night after my argument with this friend *I dreamed that I was with my ex-husband at the postal office. Suddenly I saw him walking away and disappearing. I started panicking but I told myself that I could always call his cellular phone. I grabbed my phone but the screen was broken. I asked myself when this had happened since it was a new phone. So I asked a woman next to me to lend me her phone, but when I tried dialing my ex-husband's phone number I couldn't. So I asked a third person for a phone, but when I tried dialing the phone became an accordion.* At that moment I woke up."

I couldn't but marvel at how our unconscious picks up the pieces of our waking life to put together a dream that will send us the message we need to hear. Sarah's friend had a personality very similar to Sarah's ex-husband's: egotistic, controlling, demeaning. What Sarah needed to learn is that connecting with this friend would be as difficult as it had been to connect with her ex-husband. It is also interesting to note that the oldest name for an accordion is *harmonica,* meaning harmony in Greek. So perhaps that friend needed not be in her circle of friends any more than her ex-husband needed to be in her life. What the dream was saying is that those relationships were not conducive to harmony. That is exactly what happened a couple of months later. Another argument ensued and the relationship with this friend ended. Sarah's dream had been a premonitory dream.

THINK WITH THE HEART

Many times I have been asked by patients how to react to somebody who has treated them wrong. It's true that some of us tend to be resentful and will bear grudges for a long time. However almost everybody understands that grudges are a heavy weight to carry along. They are heavy not only because they are based on anger and vindictiveness but because they separate us from others who, in one way or another, have shared our lives for a while. When Adrienne came to see me I could tell she was carrying a heavy weight on her shoulders. Her whole demeanor lacked spontaneity and her facial expression denoted irritability and perhaps even anger. It was clear to me that her life had not been easy and that she had probably suffered her share of losses and betrayals. It's true that life is all but easy. Happy moments are few and far between, and people who really love us for who we are even fewer. However, all of this has to do with learning the lessons that we came to life to learn, and it's precisely our nemeses (those who are not caring) who will become our teachers. It is only through our wounds that we become wiser. But I am getting off track. Let's go back to Adrienne, my new patient. She came to my office and sat in front of me without ever smiling. She was an attractive middle aged woman with an intelligent look. I could detect an accent so I asked her where she was from originally. "I was born in Panama but came to the States a long time ago with my now ex-husband. He came to study physics and I came along. At the time we were not yet married and decided to marry here in the United States."

I stood silent for a moment to give Adrienne the time to regroup and think about how she wanted to present her problem to me. I did not have to wait long for her to start speaking. She spoke in a very soft tone of voice, as if trying to contain the feeling of anger about to burst as she talked.

"I came to see you because I feel stuck in the past," she said. "As I mentioned before, my husband is now my ex-husband. As a matter of fact, he has been my ex-husband for quite some time now...Five years to be exact."

"Are you still grieving your divorce?" I asked.

"Not really grieving, but I am still very angry at how he lied and cheated on me," she explained.

Adrienne paused for a moment before going on.

"However, I have been feeling like this for a long time and I would like to stop being resentful."

I waited for a moment to see if my patient needed to add something, but realized that she was waiting for my comments.

"There are some losses in life that are very difficult to overcome," I started saying. "These are wounds that never heal. However, when our lives are controlled by the past we are unable to enjoy and live in the present," I added.

Adrienne looked at me with a sad expression on her face and said: "Right now I cannot enjoy any activity. What's more, I am unable to shed this deep feeling of loss that pervaded me after my divorce."

Now Adrienne was silently crying and looking for a tissue in her purse.

"I hear you," I answered. "Who hasn't felt that way at some point in life? However, there is a way to step back and start looking at your past with different eyes." I could detect a sparkle of hope in Adrienne's eyes. Was she finally going to get the key to a better life?

"How?" she asked anxiously.

"Remember that thoughts generate emotions. So you need to change the way you think about your ex-husband. Instead of seeing him as an evil person who lied and cheated on you to make you suffer, just think of him as someone who was mistreated by his caretakers and does not know any better."

"But he knew he was being dishonest"

"Yes, but that is the behavioral repertoire he learned when he was growing up. Although he knows it's wrong, he never took the time or was never able to change it."

"So I should condone his lying and his cheating."

"No, his behavior is unacceptable. What you can do is look at him with your heart and accept the fact that what happened between him and you was what needed to happen. He was one of your nemesis in this life and he came to teach you something. That is probably why you chose him as a mate. Being the way he is he could not have behaved in any other way with you or with anybody else for that matter. Take advantage of the lessons learnt and thank him for having made you wiser."

Middle Age: Our Road to Inner Wisdom

IN THE END EVERYTHING WILL BE ALRIGHT. IF IT'S NOT ALRIGHT IT'S BECAUSE IT'S NOT THE END YET

The title is not my creation. It's from the script of a wonderful movie called *"Hotel Marigold."* It is not my intention to discuss the movie at this time but rather the theory that life is wise and takes us there where we need to be. Our grandmothers used to say that unhappy events are *"blessings in disguise" or that "things happen for a reason."* The challenge has to do with the fact that until we get to "the end" we are unable to realize that, indeed, what happened was really for the better. Understanding that things happen for a reason is difficult for everybody: patients and psychotherapists, students and philosophers, laymen and religious people. Only sages can grasp this life paradigm intuitively, without needing time to reveal the secret. One of my patients, Clarissa, had to face the same challenge. Her husband had come to my office because he was dissatisfied with his marriage. He had been referred to me by another patient, whom I had been seeing for a couple of years, also for marital difficulties. Clarissa's husband (I will call him Marcelo) was an emotionally vulnerable man, who claimed to need more gestures of affection than his wife was willing to display. He said, for instance, that he would have liked to have long after dinner chats with Clarissa but that she seemed reluctant to do so and always found some excuse. Although several years have passed from that session, I still remember having thought at the time how lucky Clarissa was (I still had not met her) to have a husband who was asking for that kind of marital intimacy. After some sessions, I suggested that Marcelo bring his wife to a session so as to observe their interaction live. As soon as they set a foot in my office I realized that Clarissa had been dragged to session. Perhaps being aware that her marriage was at risk, she would have preferred not to make waves. When her husband began to complain about her coldness, she said that his personality did not encourage her to be affectionate. I asked her to give me a specific example and this is what she said: "To tell you the truth, I am reluctant to get close to my husband because when I do so he can become cold and distant. It happened to me so many times that now I am extremely cautious." She then added: "Actually, my marriage has become a relationship where I have to walk on eggshells."

I immediately understood what Clarissa meant. With a few words she provided me with the information I needed to better understand her husband: an emotionally vulnerable but distant man, unpredictable, constantly dissatisfied, with a strong tendency to blame others for his personal shortcomings, and most of all incapable of introspection. In other words: a narcissist.

Years went by and Clarissa and Marcelo's marriage ended. Marcelo went to live on his own while Clarissa stayed in the family home with their two teenage sons. While Marcelo had a couple of sessions with me after his separation, Clarissa kept coming to see me every week. Although her marriage had been very unsatisfactory during its last years, it was difficult for her to accept the fact that it was over. Clarissa was unable to accept her present reality. She couldn't understand why, after having worked hard to help her husband with his career and raised her children, her family had ceased to be. To bring her out of a past that didn't exist any longer and that had not been better, I mentioned several times that things happen for a reason and that they happen for the better. Although Clarissa agreed that if there was harmony in the universe things should follow an order, she could not really grasp the meaning of what I was saying to her. The concept of "everything is for the better" sounded logic to her but not realistic.

"Where is the proof that things happen for the better?" Clarissa asked.

My answer was that the proof only becomes evident with time. The keywords are patience and faith that we will be guided to a better place. Several months after her separation, Clarissa stopped coming to treatment. I said to myself that my interpretations of what had happened to her obviously had not helped her. Years went by and one day Clarissa called me again to make an appointment. She came to my office smiling but still with that melancholic look that I knew so well. She told me that she had met a man at a party and that they had hit it off immediately.

"It's true," she said, "I am doing well. But I still cannot understand why my family broke-up."

While listening to her I couldn't avoid thinking about that man standing on the roof of his house after a deluge and praying to God for help. After a little while a canoe came by and a man offered help. The man on the roof declined stating that he was waiting for God's help. Then a motorboat came by and a sailor offered his help. The man on the roof declined again stating that he was waiting for God's help. Finally a cruise liner came by and the captain offered help. Once again the man on the roof declined saying that he was waiting for God's help. At that moment his house went under water and before drowning the man shouted: "God, I prayed for your help and you let me down!" God answered him: "Son, I sent you a canoe and you refused to be helped; I sent you a motor boat and again you refused to be helped; I even sent you a cruise liner and you refused to be helped."

Clarissa had not yet reached the end of that journey. Although life was offering her a new beginning, she was not ready to welcome the present with a full heart. She still needed to go several miles to reach the end.

Middle Age: Our Road to Inner Wisdom

It comes a time in life when we need to let go of all the dramas and the people who provoke them. So we surround ourselves with those who make us laugh, we forget the bad moments and we remember the happy times; we love those who treat us well and we pray for those who mistreated us...

Anonymous

When Alice called me to schedule an appointment and I asked her to explain to me briefly over the phone what was the presenting problem, she answered somewhat abruptly that she would explain it to me personally. Because of her age and the urgency with which she requested an appointment I supposed that she was having marital difficulties. During middle age and after our children leave home to start their own lives, marital issues are very common. Instead, when I saw her come into my office, something told me that this patient had come to see me for a different reason. Alice was a sixty year old woman, still attractive but with a dash of sadness in her gaze. I showed her in and waited in silence for her to start telling me her story. I didn't have to wait long. Alice told me that she had been a widow for several years, that she had two grown sons and that she lived on her own.

"In the beginning and after so many years of being married, it was difficult for me to live by myself. But then I was able to make some friends and I started going out a lot."

I did not make any comments and for a moment the room was silent. I soon realized that my patient was having trouble verbalizing why she had come to see me. So I decided to give her a hand.

"You seem to have a good life," I said. "I can't imagine what brings you here." That was enough for Alice to start talking. She said that she had just come back from a trip with one of her best friends. They had known each other in a group for singles and immediately hit it off. That had been several years ago. This friend (I will call her Helen) had Alice's same age, she was divorced, and had two grown married daughters. Despite the fact that she spent a lot of time with her grandchildren, Helen used to call Alice every weekend to do something together. Although Alice had many friends that she could call, for some reason she had become very dependent on Helen's phone call. And although in the beginning the relationship had been free of conflicts, in the last year Alice started noticing that her friend had changed: she had become more irritable, she was always the one to decide where they should go, and more often than not she had spoken to Alice in a very abrupt tone of voice. At first Alice thought that her friend was going through a rough time that would soon end. But as time went by she started realizing that Helen's attitude was not a temporary situation and that she had changed for the worse. Despite this state of affairs, when her friend invited her to a trip together she immediately accepted. The day they were leaving and while she was still packing, Alice had the feeling that she was making a big mistake. Unfortunately it was too late to back off. She did not pay too much attention to her gut feelings and went on packing. Fortunately the first leg of their trip together was without any conflicts. But as days went by, Helen became gradually more irritable. That was not all. Helen started asking Alice to pay for their daily expenses and then "forgetting" to pay her back. Because planning the trip had meant a lot of work and because it was not an inexpensive itinerary, Alice decided not to quarrel and enjoy the vacation as much as possible. But when she came back home she knew that her relationship with Helen had to be revisited. That was when she decided to call me.

"What brings me here is the fact that I would hate to lose a friendship that has lasted for some years," she explained to me. "Besides, I know that we all have our flaws and that we need to be tolerant."

"Being tolerant is necessary if we don't want to end up alone," I agreed. "The problem is that there are things that we can tolerate and others that we cannot tolerate."

"And how do we know what to tolerate?"

"That is an individual decision simply because we all have different boundaries," I answered. The room was silent for a moment. I had the distinct feeling that my patient had not found my answer satisfactory. She had probably come in search of a one size fits all formula that could be applied to all cases, always.

"I am so confused that I don't know what to do," she complained. "On the one hand I am afraid of losing my friends; but on the other hand I don't want to become a people pleaser full of resentment."

"Fear is not a good counsel," I said. "Despite our fears we need to respect ourselves... Have you had any dreams lately?" For a brief moment Alice looked surprised, but then a broad smile brightened her face.

"Now that you mention it, I did have a dream. *I was in my house with two friends and we were going to sit to lunch. Because the house was very dirty, I told them that before we ate I needed to clean up. They agreed and it felt good. When everything looked sparkling clean we shared our lunch.*"

I looked at Alice and smiled. "You have just answered your question. Don't you think?"

OUR RELATIONSHIP WITH

OUR ADULT CHILDREN

One of the most complex issues of our life - should I say the most complex? - is our relationship with our children. There is a saying in Spanish that goes like this: *"Little children, little problems; older children, bigger problems."* I too have a saying: *"Once you have a child, your life does not belong to you anymore."* When a child is born the family system is completely changed. The couple stops being a dyad to become a triangle in which several dynamics start playing their roles. One of them is the deep connection between mother and child that in some way turns the father for a while into the odd man out. I still remember when my son was a newborn and my husband wanted to go out on Saturday nights, how difficult it was for me to leave the baby with a babysitter and how impatient I was to come back home. I was split between the need to be with my husband and that instinctive feeling of having to be near my newborn son, just in case he needed me. What a relief I felt to be back to that intimate connection with baby! Although for me it was an uncomfortable situation, I knew that my husband had it much worse. I am not a man but I can easily imagine what it must feel to be outside such a deep emotional bond, even for a while. Then, with time our relationship with our children necessarily changes as it goes through all the stages of life: childhood, adolescence, and adulthood. The teenage years are especially trying: since teenagers need space to grow, and many of us parents are reluctant to let them go, this is a period of conflict and distance. Gone are the days when we took our children by the hand and they tagged along, perhaps screaming and yelling, because they had no other option. Adolescence is a difficult time because it is usually based on a deep misunderstanding between parents and children. While most of us would gladly adjust to giving our children more freedom as long as they keep us informed of their whereabouts, our children misunderstand our need for information for need to control. As a result, a lot of them refuse to communicate with us and in return we become more inflexible and controlling. Fortunately, and as Heraclitus would remind us, nothing stays the same and suddenly we are confronted with another change: our children are already eighteen and ready to move out. The day our children leave for college -and we know it is usually going to be for many years- we suddenly realize how fast they have grown. Like in those moments just before death, we can see flashes of our life with them in a split second and we regret perhaps not having been more patient with their struggle for independence. Now, off they go and even when they come back to visit during the holidays, our relationship with them is necessarily different, perhaps less intimate, and always tinged with a little nostalgic sadness. Then they graduate and we look at them in awe like we would at a work of art; an achievement that has to do with them, with us and with the universe. It is at that moment that our children become our adult children. Remember the Spanish saying at the beginning of this post? *Older children: bigger problems.* That was the case with Corina, a divorced middle aged woman with an adult professional son. She came to see me not because the relationship between them was conflictive. On the contrary: it was too good. Because she did not have a partner, Corina had become co-dependent on her son. Although she worked as a computer analyst and had plenty of friends to go out with, her main interest in life was her son. She waited impatiently for his phone calls and for the moments where she could see him. She decided to come see me after a conversation during which her son had been rude to her. After hanging up the phone with him she became frantic, almost to the point of a panic attack. She described her feeling to me as standing on a cliff, with her son emotionally far away and indifferent to her. It was an unbearable feeling of loneliness and emptiness. In our therapy sessions we explored her inability to handle conflict with her son in a healthy way, and her sensation of him vanishing from her life completely when he was not present. Was it related to her own mother's indifference when she was a baby? Babies are very sensitive to their environmental cues and how the world reacts towards them. John Bowlby based his attachment theory on how tolerantly and understandingly children are accepted by their caretakers. During the course of therapy Corina came to realize that this had not happened in her childhood, and that the attachment between her and her mother had been fragile at best. She lacked object constancy: people existed only if she could see them. Corina had transferred this feeling of abandonment from her mother to her son, with the result that whenever they had a conflict she felt as if he would vanish from her life. When Corina was able to grasp the fact that the feeling of abandonment was a projection that had nothing to do with reality (as a matter of fact, her son was very caring with her), I encouraged her to start becoming more emotionally independent from him. We decided to try a behavioral approach by her not calling him that often and spacing their encounters at least for a while. Although in the beginning it was very difficult for her to follow my suggestions, she was finally able to put more interest in her own work and social life and depend less on her son's attention. I never got to meet Corina's son but I have no doubt that he sensed the difference in his mother's attitude towards him and felt relieved. In one of our last sessions I asked Corina what was different in her relationship with her son now that therapy was about to end. Without even thinking she smiled at me and said: "I have regrouped. I am finally myself."

EVERYTHING FLOWS

HERACLITUS

Pema Chodron's book *The Places that Scare You* reminded me of Heraclitus famous quote about life's fluidity. In her book, the author mentions the three characteristics of human existence that according to the Buddha are impermanence, egolessness and suffering. Whenever I read about the Buddhist view of life I can't avoid being surprised by the fact that although it is evident that everything in the universe flows, we human beings feel in general a deep aversion for change. Furthermore, we are poorly equipped to understand that the only thing we really possess is the present moment. As a matter of fact, Pema Chodron talks about her gratitude to the Buddha for teaching us that the people and the situations in our lives are totally unpredictable: one day they are here, the next they are gone. It is only our tendency to try to control the events of our lives and our need for permanence what generates our existential suffering. According to Pema Chodron our life is really in a permanent state of transition (a paradox indeed!) where almost nothing falls under our control. Our main spiritual task should be to learn how to feel comfortable with the concept of impermanence. I have to admit that Pema Chodron's book made me feel anxious: the author definition of human existence excludes any kind of refuge. In other words, the spiritual task of every human being should be not only to adapt to the idea of constant change but also to question everything, even the spiritual theories that sustain our view of the universe. That is why the Buddha reminded those willing to listen that they should not follow his path but should find their own path instead. *Look at the moon, not at the finger pointing at the moon*.* However, the lack of solidity of phenomena is not all negative, since not only the good moments of our lives flow but also the sad ones. This paradigm is extremely useful in cases of prolonged depression. Depression feeds itself mainly on negative mental schemata, like for instance, that nothing will ever change and that our life will stay exactly the way it is now. Not exactly what Heraclitus believed! I remember the case of Cari, a middle age woman who came to see me after her divorce because she had been unable to shed the sadness that had stayed with her after her marital breakup.

"I wake up in the morning and I have difficulties getting out of bed," she told me.

"What is your first thought in the morning, when you wake up?" I asked her.

"That nothing has meaning, that nothing will ever change..."

Cari was at the time 65 years old. At her age she was still attractive and interesting, but lonely. Our therapeutic goal during six months was to reframe her negative mental schemata and to instill in Cari the notion that things change, that nothing stays the same, ever. When a patient in Cari's situation comes to therapy, by and general she will spend hours talking about the past and how things could be different today if only she had done or not done certain things. These patients are also hoping that the therapist will say things like: "How do you know that your love life is over?" The patients' loneliness and despair can become a trap for the therapist since it is very tempting to comfort them by instilling the hope that the broken relationship can be mended or that a new prince charming will appear soon. In my case I try to avoid playing astrologer. My therapeutic goal in cases like this consists in putting past and future into perspective and help patients overcome their depression not through easy optimism but by adjusting to the changes in their lives. Life is unpredictable and we never know what awaits us. However, in a society that values appearances so much, the options for a middle age woman of finding another partner are definitely scarce. From my point of view it is better to face the fact that there are great possibilities that a patient like Cari will end up living her life alone than instill in her unrealistic expectations. In my therapeutic work to overcome this kind of loss I prefer to focus on the importance of enjoying the present moment with all it has to offer rather than focusing on the future. In this kind of situation Heraclitus' quote comes in handy and helps patients clear the past of its exaggerated importance. Our mind can play tricks on us by getting us stuck in the past when really our past does not exist anymore and we are no longer the people we were. Not even our body is the same since our cells are constantly regenerating. It is only when we realize that the only thing we really possess is the present (the future is only based on speculations) that we can start to turn the page on that past forever and focus on enjoying the now. Transforming our tendency of anchoring ourselves in the past is not an easy task. We are creatures of habit and all that is new generates fear as well as a feeling of emptiness and anxiety, especially because change is also loss. Facing change and impermanence requires courage and faith that life will take us where we need to go. When we look at our lives we need to understand that despite the pain of our losses, the changes in our lives have been necessary changes. It's precisely those painful changes the ones that instill in us the wisdom that we need to acquire. If we are able to accept and adapt to change, our life will flow without interruptions. Otherwise it will stay forever stuck in a past that has ceased to exist.

*Zen saying

JUST REMEMBER THE HAPPY MOMENTS AND MOVE ON

The other night I was watching a Romanian movie, *The Day Before Christmas*, about a married man who falls for his daughter's young dentist. Although the story is not something we have never heard about before, the movie script reflects very well the characters' psychological meanders. The acting is also very convincing. Even the young actress who plays the daughter seems to have been able to easily immerse herself in her role. When the movie starts, the husband's affair with the younger woman has been dragging for months, but he does not seem ready yet to break up his marriage....until the day before Christmas, when he decides to tell his wife that he has fallen in love with another woman. The scene where the husband confesses to his wife that he is in love with somebody else is heart breaking, not only because the wife never suspected that her husband was cheating (as a matter of fact, they seem to have a pretty stable marriage), but because she feels and says to him that he has ruined her life. For some reason these words stayed in my mind long after I had finished watching the movie, perhaps because in their simplicity they verbalize a desperate feeling of loss. The husband's confession as well as his decision to leave the marriage faced the wife in a split second with the loneliness that occurs when a marital relationship is broken. The spectator first reaction to this kind of statement is of course that it is exaggerated and that with time the wife, who is still young, will be able to recover from her loss and start over. However, her words are not merely words yelled in a moment of rage. I definitely believe that the sense of a lost future is real and that those who have gone through this kind of situation know it well. Whenever I had to deal with one of these crises at the office, I have to admit that I was at a loss in finding words that would reflect my patients' feelings accurately, especially if the patient was a middle age woman. After having invested so many years in a marriage and in raising the children, to reach a point in life where instead of reaping the benefits of such hard work a woman is told by her husband that he wants out is a pill extremely difficult to swallow. Like one patient recently told me: "This kind of betrayal is like inviting my best friend home and realizing that she stole money from my purse." As a therapist, it was very stressful for me to find words to relieve in some way the deep suffering that my clients were going through with their loss. It took me many years of practice and many stories of betrayal to find the words that would allow me to reach my patients' heart. I understood that in order to overcome this pain it was necessary to reframe the situation in a more positive way. I sensed that my patients' main goal should be to avoid hating their partner. We all know that hating another only hurts ourselves and holds us stuck in the past. So after dedicating several sessions to reviewing the presenting problem in detail, I gave my patients a task: to retrieve an old photo album and spend several days looking at pictures of happier times. Connecting to their partners through happy memories would allow my patients to understand that the person they had fallen in love with was the one in the pictures, not the one that had betrayed and abandoned them. The latter was just a stranger. If we look at our life conflicts from this point of view, our resentment towards those who harmed us will disappear and instead we will need to thank them for the shared happy moments. I have to admit that few were the patients who could internalize and accept this paradigm, perhaps because we human beings are more used to feeling rage than to forgive. I never failed to emphasize that the hurt my patients had been inflicted was real and that it would always stay in their heart, no matter how much water would flow under the bridge. However, their resentment need not be there if they understood that only forgiveness can open the door of our private hell.

GOD GRANT ME THE SERENITY TO ACCEPT THE THINGS I CANNOT CHANGE; THE COURAGE TO CHANGE THE THINGS I CAN, AND THE WISDOM TO KNOW THE DIFFERENCE.

R. NEIBUHR

A couple of weeks ago, a middle aged woman --I will call her Estelle-- came to my office with issues of depression. She had been divorced for four years and was starting to become concerned about the fact that hers appeared to be a prolonged grief reaction. Her husband of 27 years had left her to marry a younger woman because, as he put it, he wanted a new shot at life. My client, now 59, was finding it very difficult to adjust to her new reality. Although her relationship with her now ex-husband had not been excellent, they had made a good team raising two wonderful daughters, working and saving money for retirement, as well as achieving a certain social status in the town where they lived. Estelle's story confirmed once again the fact that "silver haired divorce" is on the rise and probably linked to the fact that nowadays people live much longer. Once the children are gone, many marriages are left empty of common goals and meaning. Although I believe that in some cases a divorce is a good way out of a stagnant situation, sometimes people fail to understand that even good marriages have periodic crises. As the Chinese logograph of the word explains it, a crisis is the crucial moment in time when something starts to shift. The word is composed of two sino-characters: danger and opportunity. A certain situation starts to change and provides us with the opportunity to change as well. For many of us, especially if we have been living with a mate who has become distant, unmotivated, and sometimes even hostile, our first reaction is to start envisioning a new life with somebody else. Unfortunately, finding another middle aged mate who fits our bill is nowadays so complicated that not even movies depict these happy endings anymore. What happens most of the time is that the mate who left hoping to build a new and happier life ends up regretting that move forever. This is what I told a grieving Estelle.

"It's possible," she said. "But knowing this is not enough to heal the wound my husband left in my heart."

That much I knew, but I just wanted to dispel the idea that most of us have that other people's lives are happier than ours. Each of us struggles with life crises, no matter how rich or how famous or how beautiful we might be. On her second session I asked Estelle to buy a journal so that she could start writing down daily notes about her feelings, about her dreams, and about the thoughts that triggered her depression. Estelle agreed and the following session she came with a notebook that had the Alcoholics Anonymous mantra on the cover: "*God grant me the serenity to accept the things I cannot change; the courage to change the things I can; and the wisdom to know the difference.*" Since I knew that Estelle did not have any substance abuse issues, I asked her what had prompted her to buy that notebook. She explained that she knew that without the belief in a Higher Power she would not be able to change her life around in any way shape or form. She had to convince herself that the things that had happened in her life had a purpose, that she had divine protection, and that with time she would understand why she had been tested that way. Since I am a spiritual person I also believe that everything that happens in our lives happens for a reason. In my own moments of crisis I have always felt a transcendent presence near me helping me make the right choices, inducing me to call the right person, and motivating me to read the right books. Armed with knowledge drawn from my own life experience and from my patients' experience, I started guiding Estelle in her new journey. By writing every day about her thoughts and feelings, her journal became her link to her unconscious processes. She started to know herself better and gradually the events in her life became clearer. After reading her notes she came to see how her husband's decision to leave had also been her decision to let him go. She was not a victim of her circumstances but someone who had been an active participant in the events of her life. It was this understanding that brought about the acceptance of what had happened as well as the serenity she was craving for.

LIVE OUR LIFE ACCORDING TO PREFERENCES OR PRINCIPLES?

The other day I was listening to my car radio. Suddenly, while I was looking for a classical music station, a Christian station popped up. The pastor was talking about how to live the life of a good Christian. Since I wasn't very interested in the subject I decided to keep looking for music. I was about to change stations when I suddenly heard the preacher ask the audience a question: *"Should we live life according to our preferences or according to our principles?"* His question caught my attention, especially because I had asked myself the same question innumerable times. At that moment I remembered how often some patients had asked me if they or their partners had the right to break up a marriage that made them unhappy. By and general the question had to do with someone having or not the right to dissolve a marital contract knowing that by doing so a fellow human being would suffer. I had always thought that a question like this had many answers. On the one hand, it can be said that marriage is similar to a mortgage and that once we sign the contract we do not stop making our monthly payments just because we don't like the house anymore. On the other hand, it could be argued that the house can be sold and the mortgage paid off so as to buy a new house. There is however a difference between a mortgage and a marital contract: houses are made of bricks but people have feelings. When a family dissolves it's not only the children who suffer the consequences. Everybody goes through the trauma. We can be certain of one thing: it is impossible to build our happiness over the pain and the sorrow of others. The negative energy generated by the pain that we inflict on other people does not dissolve nor does it disappear. It continues pervading our life and creating hurdles. *Nothing disappears, it only changes.** It is true that a marriage, especially a long term marriage, deteriorates with time and cohabitation; and that when children leave home we sometimes feel tempted to divorce and look for new beginnings. In the vast majority of cases it is usually one partner who decides to leave while the other partner suffers from being left behind. The one who stays is usually convinced that unless the marriage is abusive and dangerous, in the great majority of cases crises can be negotiated and solved. The only condition is that both partners need to be motivated to make concessions and to understand that each one has a different world view. If we have the ability to meet our partners halfway and if we put their needs at the same level we put ours, marriage becomes a team as well as a satisfying life situation. In the world we live right now, more women than men start divorce proceedings. This is probably because more men tend to engage in affairs than women. Perhaps they don't see the option of renegotiating a new marital contract. If we accept that our partners are independent human beings, with their own personality traits and their own needs and goals (and not people who were born to satisfy all our needs), not only can we solve our differences but also our marriage can become like a refuge. A marriage, like any other relationship, should only dissolve after all options of reconciliation have been explored and tried out. When the pastor mentioned the difference between living according to our principles versus living according to our preferences I thought about how much easier it is to just decide on the basis of what we like. However, as I mentioned many times before, life's purpose is not to be happy but to become wiser. In our daily struggle our choices play a very significant role. Jean Paul Sartre mentioned that *"I am my choices."* I could add that our individual choices will reverberate in the whole universe and contribute to its evolution. In other words: our choices are the legacy we leave behind. We need to ask ourselves what we want our legacy to be. It is true that living by our principles is much more demanding and difficult. But at the end of the day, if we make the effort to live ethically the rewards will benefit not just us but the whole universe.

*The discovery of the conservation of mass by Antoine Lavoisier

WHEN THE STUDENT IS READY THE TEACHER APPEARS.

BUDDHIST SAYING

The first time I read this statement, a long time ago, I was certain that one day I would meet a very wise and learned person to whom I could ask all those questions that I was unable to answer by myself. In other words, the teacher would be a fellow human being that would teach me the difficult art of living wisely. It did not occur to me at the time that nobody who is not me can teach me how to live my own life. This was proven to me once again by one of my patients, whom I shall call Sonia. Sonia was a middle age professional woman who had been married for many years and had decided to separate from her husband when she realized that she could not communicate with him anymore. For some reason, with the passage of time he had become more avoidant and almost impossible to reach. Although she had been the one to take the first step five years ago, Sonia had been unable to shed the deep feeling of loneliness that had pervaded her life after her divorce. Despite having a good job and a nurturing group of friends, she still longed for the marriage she had had to break up. She was so desperate for fast answers that before coming to see me she had consulted a professional astrologer who was also a psychotherapist. Since the astrologer lived in another state, the session took place over the phone and it was basically the explanation of Sonia's natal chart. Later, when Sonia shared with me her impressions, she said that it had surprised her how accurate the astrologer had been in describing her childhood as well as her personality traits. However, what had impressed her most of all was that the astrologer had told her that she was now entering a new life stage in which she would have some extra-sensorial experiences. When Sonia asked her what kind of extra-sensorial experiences the astrologer answered that she would start having premonitory dreams. It was difficult for Sonia to believe this statement due to the fact that during the five years after her marital separation she had barely dreamed. Her sleep was constantly interrupted and she always felt tired. So as time went by she forgot all about the astrology session. Then one day, a few days before her birthday, her former husband called her to request a document.

Before he ended the conversation he told her that he would call her again to wish her a happy birthday. Needless to say, this conversation had a profound effect on Sonia. Once again it made her envision her life as a couple. No more feelings of loneliness or the daily need to go out into the world looking for companionship. It's true, she remembered, that her husband was a difficult man and that a relationship with him would bring a lot of disruption into her life. But would that be worse than no relationship at all, she asked herself? If they were together, at least they could work on improving their communication. The night before her birthday Sonia felt very tired and went to sleep early. That night she had a strange dream. She dreamed *that she had to call her husband before a certain time but that she did not have a phone. Although she was among several people, nobody would lend her a phone. Finally she found a woman who was willing to let her use hers but when she tried to dial, she was unable to do so. Desperate, she thought how angry her husband would be for her not calling him.* On the day of her birthday, when her husband called her she was talking to a friend. She took his call and told him that she would call him later. Less than two minutes later she returned his call but he did not answer the phone. She called him again to no avail. At this point Sonia remembered her dream and understood its meaning: that the vision of togetherness with her husband was just that, a vision. When Sonia told me this incident during one of our therapy sessions I was amazed at how the dream had foreseen exactly what would happen the next day. But what most impressed me was that Sonia remembered it and understood it. In other words, the teaching had taken place when the student was ready.

COINCIDENCES OR DIVINE SYNCHRONICITY?

We are always told that God works in mysterious ways and that we need to trust how our life unfolds. No matter how difficult the situation we are in, sooner or later life will show us that we are always where we need to be. For those of us who believe in the perfection of the Universe, this knowledge infuses us with the strength to bear what comes our way. When the going gets rough hope is what helps us reach the other shore. On the contrary, if hopelessness pervades us, our life becomes a dark unending tunnel. I have always been a spiritual person who never doubted that there is a Power greater than myself present in my life. It has always been my impression that the reality that we see is not the whole story. *"There is more than meets the eye."* Through the years I was lucky enough to perceive in my own life some unequivocal signs of a divine presence. Actually, I am sure that these signs appear in the lives of all of us; it's just a matter of paying attention. In my case, I took a note of the signs that materialized in my life so as to retrieve them when a new crisis would pop up and I needed to feel safe again. Today I want to share one of those markers with my readers because I know it will help others have faith in life. This event took place some years ago while I was having lunch with a group of colleagues in front of my office building. At that time I felt very frustrated with my job because of a supervisor that had been hired some time before. He was young and inexperienced and his favorite hobby was to micromanage all of us no end. His managing style had become our daily torment. That day a group of us decided to go to lunch to a cafeteria in front of our building. It was a huge eatery with some tables placed outside. The month was May and the weather was so relaxing that we decided to sit at the only empty table left on the curb. The restaurant was a self-service buffet so we had to take turns to go get our food, and since I was not very hungry I let the others go first. While I was waiting for my colleagues to come back with their trays, I decided to close my eyes like I would at the beach. It felt like a marvelous feeling of freedom in the middle of a busy workday, so much so that for a moment I stopped being aware of my surroundings. Suddenly I heard somebody asking me for directions in French. I opened my eyes and saw in front of me a tall Haitian woman all covered in sweat and very agitated. I looked at her and then looked around and saw that although the place was crowded, for some reason she had chosen me to help her. Most than anything else I wanted to ask her how she knew that I spoke

French, but didn't. She looked too distraught and in need of help fast.

"I am lost," she said. "I am looking for this address," she added handing me a piece of paper.

I looked at the address and asked around if anyone knew where it was located. A couple of young men at the table near me gave me some directions that I proceeded to explain to her. I told her that the address she was looking for was near but not at walking distance and asked her if she had transportation. She said that she did not and looked at me in anguish.

"I just came to Miami from Haiti and was lucky enough to get a job interview at a warehouse," she explained. "I need to be there by 1pm," she gasped.

By then it was 12.45pm. I looked at her and sensed her quiet desperation. I knew how I would be feeling if with fifteen minutes left for a job interview I would not know where to turn. She kept looking at me without daring to ask me to take her wherever she needed to go, and although I was well aware of the dangers of transporting a stranger in my car in Miami, I felt I had no options.

"I'll take you," I told her. I knew I was doing the right thing.

After telling my colleagues where I was headed, I walked towards my car with her. We drove for about ten minutes until we finally got to the location of her interview. Before getting out of the car she said to me:

"God will reward you for what you have done today."

I wished her luck in the interview and went back to the office. A week after this incident, I was having lunch at the office kitchen when one of my colleagues came in and started looking for her food in the refrigerator. I had known this colleague for many years because we had worked together on several occasions in the past. She was as unhappy with her current position as I was, but she had decided to resign and start her own practice. She sat next to me and started eating her meal.

"AG has an opening for a new position in Miami. Did you see it?" She asked me matter of fact.

"How do you know?" I almost screamed.

"It's posted on ABC.com. Why don't you apply?"

I had been wishing to work for AG for so long that I could hardly believe my ears. Many years ago they had offered me a position that I had refused because my priority at that time was to take care of my family. Now I did not have that responsibility anymore and I was dreaming to work for a company like AG. Without finishing my lunch I went back to my computer, logged into ABC.com and applied for the position online. That was on a Wednesday. By Friday the recruiter had already called me to schedule an interview and two weeks later I was hired. Needless to say I still think about the Haitian woman's blessing. However, what most impressed me was the fact that had I gone to the office kitchen to have lunch at a different time, I would not have met the colleague who gave me the position information. By the same token, perhaps the Haitian woman also asked herself once and again how did she guessed that I spoke French. We could view these events as the result of a coincidence. I prefer to view them as Divine synchronicity

GO WITH THE FLOW

HERACLITUS

I was listening the other day to an interview to a psychoanalyst from South America. The leitmotiv of the conversation was that sooner or later pain and loss make their entrance in every home and that we need to adjust to it and move on. I would even go further and say that most of life's problems are generated by our difficulty in adapting to change and loss. Already Heraclitus of Ephesus, a pre-Socratic Greek philosopher, stated in the fifth century BC that we *"cannot step into the same river twice."* By the same token, in a more recent historical time the Diagnostic and Statistical Manual of Mental Disorders (also known as DSM-V) dedicates a section to what is called Adjustment Disorders. These are disorders that have to do with our lack of adaptation to changes in our life. With no doubt, change is stressful for most of us. Why is it so difficult to adapt to life changes? By and general, changes have to do with the loss of what is known and familiar. I remember reading a long time ago *Necessary Losses* by Judith Viorst, a book that opened my eyes to the sad fact that life is indeed an exercise in flexibility and acceptance. In other words, life's main goal consists of none other than the difficult task of accepting impermanence. The Buddha made impermanence the basis of his teachings. We all tend to feel more secure in a familiar environment and among familiar faces. For the majority of us unknown situations and strange people spell danger. Nowhere like in the second part of life is loss and change more significant and painful. As a therapist, I can attest that a great majority of the clients who come to see me are middle aged people who are desperately trying to adapt to profound changes in their lives. One of these patients, Odile, comes to mind, not because her problems were different from those of other women's problems but because she had a more difficult time adapting to the losses and changes in her life. She had been referred to me by one of my oldest patients, who was her childhood friend. Odile had been married for 35 years to a doctor and had raised 3 children. She did not have a profession so when the children started going to school she decided to do some volunteer work with the terminally ill. Between her family duties and her husband's social engagements Odile did not even realize that as time went by her marriage was falling apart. Seasons came and went and when the last of their children left for college, Odile's husband confessed to her that he was gay and that he had been in love with a man for more than 4 years. Now that the children were no longer at home, he said, the time had come for him to end a lifestyle that was basically dishonest. Although Odile had suspected for a while that her husband was having an affair, never in her wildest dreams did she think it was with another man. The fact that she had been married for so many years to a homosexual faced Odile with the harrowing task of finding out who she really was and why she had made the choices that she had. Her children, on the other hand, also had a difficult time adapting to the idea of having a gay father, which made her process of adaptation even more complicated. When Odile came to see me, four years had elapsed since her ex-husband had confessed to her his sexual orientation. Immediately after the breakup Odile had gone to see a psychiatrist to be prescribed an antidepressant, but she had been reluctant to see a therapist. Starting to explore uncharted territory was too scary at that time and she decided to postpone the therapy. However, as time went by she became increasingly depressed and irritable, mainly because she was unable to accept that life as she knew it was forever gone and that she had no choice but to rebuild a new life for herself. When she came to see me we spent many sessions talking about her difficulty in adjusting to the reality of her current situation. Even her body, with frequent stomach aches, was sending her the message that she had to learn to digest what life had faced her with. From an intellectual point of view Odile understood perfectly well that she had no other option than to look in front of her and start a new life journey. However, emotionally she continued to turn her head towards her past and dreamed of magical solutions.

"The person you fell in love with doesn't exist anymore," I told her once in session. "Even the person you were at that time no longer exists."

She knew I was right but reality was too painful to accept and the past even more difficult to let go of. Finally, many hours of therapy later Odile was able to get to grips with the idea that the changes that had happened in her life needed to happen. Those situations were not isolated events but part of the whole tapestry of her existence.

"We can resist change with all our might, but it's eventually useless," I told her once in session. "If we don't make the necessary changes ourselves, life will make them for us. Going with the flow of life will help us focus on what we have and not on what we have lost.

HELL IS OTHERS

"No Exit", J.P. SARTRE

When Sandra came to my office it was apparent that she was going through a very rough time. However, despite her sad demeanor and her anxiety she was an interesting middle age woman who did not have any difficulties verbalizing her pain and, at times, her anger. Sandra had been married for 26 years to a man who had become very successful. Despite being an accountant, most of the time Sandra had only worked part-time because she wanted to take care of her daughter. Meanwhile her husband had invested most of his energy in building an internet site that had become a success and had made them very rich. As many women I know Sandra had devoted her life to her family and had especially being there for her husband when he needed a partner to build up his social network. In other words, she had stretched herself thin in order to meet her daughter's and her husband's needs. Despite the fact that she was now separated from her husband she made it clear to me that she never regretted having being there for them. "Things don't always work out the way we want them to," she said with a sigh. "But I did not come to see you to talk about what I would have liked my husband to be."

In listening to Sandra I remember thinking that it was not very often that I heard a patient talk that way. Patients usually come to see me to complain about how reality is different from what they want reality to be. I immediately sensed that this would be a different kind of therapeutic encounter, one in which I would perhaps have to delve deep into my philosophical view of the world.

"I am here to talk about an incident that happened to me with one of my friends and that made me think that life is indeed a lonely journey," she said. "A long time ago, when I was a teenager, a friend said to me that people don't really love you. At that time I thought her statement was an exaggeration perhaps due to her life experiences and that it could not be applied to all people. Now, many years later, I can't avoid thinking that she was right. What do you think? Was she right?"

The question caught me off guard especially because I had been tackling with the same issue for some time.

"It's a good question," I answered to buy time. "Why don't you tell me what happened to you so that we can think together and, perhaps, reach a conclusion that will feel comfortable for you."

Sandra agreed and proceeded to tell me that after her husband had moved out of their home, she had gone on a trip to see her family who lived in a South American country. Besides her family, she had met with friends, some of them friends she had known through her ex-husband and with whom she had become fairly close. One day the wife of her ex-husband's childhood friend invited her to lunch, but before going to the restaurant she had asked her if she minded that they go visit the studio of a painter friend of hers. Sandra readily agreed and when they got there her friend's friend came to greet them. At that moment, her friend looked at her and instead of introducing her to the painter she asked: "How do I introduce you? What name should I use?" Sandra was flabbergasted. Not only she had always used her husband's last name but also she had not even started divorce proceedings yet. Sandra paused for a moment and looked at me as if waiting for me to say something. I was silent because I know that there are situations in life that cannot be described with words; the pain is just too deep and it's better to observe and listen intently. Sandra went on.

"At that time I had just separated from my husband and had a lot of difficulty accepting the fact that he was gone," she said. "I had accepted the invitation of this friend thinking that it would be an opportunity to share my pain and be comforted by her. On the contrary, I found myself having lunch with the enemy. I even got a terrible cramp on my neck," she added.

Needless to say I was still at a loss for words. When the pain is so deep, words are useless.

"Did you tell her that you were upset and that she knew your name perfectly well?" I asked after a while.

"No. I was so distraught that I was afraid to start crying, and I didn't want to give her satisfaction. I just went ahead and introduced myself." Sandra went on to tell me that during lunch this friend had made comments about how she had told her husband that he should also try to build an internet site and become rich like Sandra's husband.

"I was so surprised by her comments that I did not know what to make of them. It's so hard for me to think that she acted that way out of envy."

After countless hours of therapy with patients as well as from my own life experience I can definitely say that envy is a very generalized feeling, especially among those individuals whose life has not turned out the way they thought it should have. Envious people are people who relish the fact that other people have fallen from life's grace and for one reason or another are going through a rough time. I am sure that many of them are ashamed of feeling that way towards others, but it's obvious that they go through a sort of catharsis when they see that others are as unhappy as they are. That is why they can't avoid making comments like Sandra's friend who needed to point out to her that her husband was not her husband any longer.

"Some people are like that," I said. "Not everybody. You need to focus on those people who can give you a hand in times of need and let go of the others."

Sandra looked at me sadly but relieved. It probably felt good that another human being, especially a therapist, seemed to have gone through the same experience.

"Some people live very shallow lives and constantly compare themselves to others who seem to fare better," I said. "They don't understand that they need to focus on themselves and that envying other people's karma will not help them evolve. It's simply a waste of time."

Sandra agreed with me. I could feel that I had given her a key to start closing that chapter of her life. Her ex-husband, his friends and his friends' wives were not a part of her life anymore. She needed to bless them and let them go. The time had come for her to remember her childhood friend's statement and only surround herself with those who deserved her company.

IS IT TRUE? IS IT COMPASSIONATE?

DOES IT HAVE ANY PURPOSE?

BUDDHIST SAYING

Right speech is the third precept of the Buddhist Noble Eightfold Path and it has to do with the words we use when we address others. We all know how powerful words can be in certain situations. As a matter of fact words can sometimes be used as daggers to intentionally or unintentionally hurt a fellow human being. Despite being aware of the danger of using words incorrectly, in our daily life we oftentimes forget how harsh and hurtful they can be. The subject was raised in session by one of my patients, Chiara, who was just recovering from a long and harrowing divorce process. Chiara had been married for 25 years to Marcello, a 57 year old businessman whose sense of entitlement made living with him very difficult. They had both met in their country of origin in Europe in their twenties after having been introduced by a common friend. At that time life was easier not only because they did not have any major responsibilities, but because when we are young our personality pathology (if we have one) has not yet fully developed. At that time Marcello was a computer science graduate looking for work while Chiara was still struggling to complete her medical studies. She still had a year to go to finish her residence in psychiatry and she was specializing in children and adolescents. In session Chiara spoke of those first years of her relationship with Marcello as some of the happiest years of her life. Although having different personalities, what she remembered most vividly was how both of them had similar views on many subjects and how happy were the weekends they spent together. Chiara was totally in love with Marcello and convinced that she had found the man of her dreams. It is true, she explained, that sometimes Marcello had reacted with disproportionate anger to some situations, but she was so much in love with her husband that she could hardly pay any attention to those warning signs. One day in session I asked her to describe to me one of Marcello's angry outbursts. She proceeded to tell me the following episode.

"We had just moved to the United States and a notice came that our furniture had arrived from overseas and was waiting to be picked up at the US Customs. At that time our first child was only 2 years old and we decided that Marcello would ask a work colleague to help him while I stayed home with our daughter. At around lunchtime Marcello and his friend arrived home with the cargo. After parking the truck in front of the house, Marcello stormed inside and started yelling at me for delegating on him that kind of an errand. He should not be moving furniture in a truck, he said, and on top of everything else he was due back to work in an hour. His friend and I listened in silence, almost in a state of shock, not knowing exactly what to make of Marcello's disproportionate reaction. It was obvious that during his trip back home with the cargo for some reason Marcello had been ruminating about being taken advantage of by me and exploded as soon as he arrived home. The fact is that the joy of receiving all our belongings and being able to start living in a more comfortable and familiar environment was ruined by this inexplicable reaction."

As she recalled this incident Chiara started to cry silently, not so much for an episode that had happened so many years ago but for all the similar hurtful words spoken by Marcello in the years that followed.

Time went by and with the boom of websites Marcello became a very successful and wealthy businessman. However, and as is usually the case, wealth did not come alone. As Marcello stated in the course of one of their marital sessions: "Money does indeed cause a lot of problems."

Like in many other similar marital situations where the husband becomes financially powerful, Marcello started spending more time at the office and less time at home. Although Chiara was also professionally successful, her priority had always been her family and as such she had spent a lot more time with her children than her husband. Almost without being aware of it, they both started distancing from each other to the point where Marcello initiated an extramarital relationship with his assistant.

Needless to say, when Chiara found out that her husband was unfaithful she was devastated and without the shadow of a doubt she decided to file for divorce. As she explained to me in session, her marriage had become so stagnant and her husband so distant that she did not have the energy to try to fix it anymore. After the divorce was final and her children left for college, Chiara turned her attention to what she had left: her profession. One day she was attending a seminar at a nearby hospital and ran into a colleague that she had not seen in a while. Her colleague waved at her when the seminar was just starting, but at the first break came walking towards her.

"Hey, long time no see," her colleague greeted her.

"Hello there," answered Chiara.

"I see that you are working at XX Hospital," was her friend's comment.

"That's right and very happy about it" Chiara agreed.

"Listen... Are you still married?" asked her colleague lowering her voice.

"No, I divorced Marcello three years ago. I went through difficult times and had no choice," explained Chiara with a little tremor in her voice.

"I thought so because I saw something..." said her colleague with no further explanation.

Chiara still remembers vividly what she felt at that moment.

"It was as if a sharp object had pierced my heart," she explained one day to me in session crying as if the event had happened the day before. "I am not speaking metaphorically." she added quickly. "I felt the metal inside my body."

She did not have to convince me. I know how words can hurt as we all have gone through this kind of experience when others have spoken hurtful words without sometimes even being aware of the consequences. I often wonder what is needed to make us aware of the tremendous power of words. If each of us would be mindful of how we talk to those around us our relationship with them, even our most difficult relationships, would not become the battlefields they sometimes are. We just need to keep in mind the Buddha precepts about right speech and we will avoid inflicting unnecessary harm on our fellow human beings.

1. Is it true?
2. Is it compassionate?
3. Does it serve any purpose?

If the answer is no we should keep our comments to ourselves.

JUNGIAN SHADOW AND KARMA

*"Without the conscious inclusion of the shadow in daily life there cannot be a positive relationship to other people, or to the creative sources in the soul; there cannot be an individual relationship to the Divine."** The shadow lies deep inside of us. It consists of all those traits that are outside our consciousness and that we repudiate or that we fear. It's the wrinkles we do not want to see on our face when we look at ourselves in the mirror. A soft light will definitely make us look better; however wrinkles will still be there waiting to be acknowledged. But it would be a mistake to describe the Jungian shadow only in negative terms. Being a side of our personality, the shadow needs to be made conscious and it only becomes a negative factor when repressed. What I mean by negative factor is that whatever we ignore about ourselves will sooner or later face us from the outside. In our relationships we will project our shadow so that others will act out for us what we don't dare carry out ourselves. For Jung the shadow had to do with the individual as well as with the collective unconscious. While our individual shadow

unfolds in our daily life, our collective shadow will unfold in periods of historical upheaval like during a war or in times of violence like the ones we are living currently. A shadow that is ignored will be a ghost always meddling in our affairs with others in such a way that none of our relationships, especially the most intimate ones, will be authentic. In other words, we will not be relating to other human beings for who they really are but to what we have projected unto them from our unconscious. Helena came to see me following the advice of a friend. She was 52 at the time. A very friendly and good looking woman, Helena told me that she had been married for 22 years to a very successful doctor. They had one son who was also in medical school and living on his own. After their son had left, both Helena and her then husband decided that they would try to live separately for a while to try to work on their issues which they had not been able to solve in therapy and which had become especially thorny after their son had left for college. So they did. While Helena stayed in the family home, her husband moved to an apartment they had bought to rent seasonally. Once the husband moved out of the home however, he became increasingly distant and not really willing to work on their marital issues. After so many years of cohabitation, it was evident that he was avid of freedom and new adventures. As she gradually realized that her husband's suggestion of "living together separately" had been a mere excuse to get out of the marriage, Helena became severely depressed, so much so that I suggested that she go see a psychiatrist for medication. Helena followed my advice and although she did not feel overwhelmed with joy, after a while she definitely was able to regroup. The energy to work on her issues of grief and loss came back and she started seeing the light at the end of the tunnel. Helena's story was not new to me. Hers was the typical story of the husband who reaches middle age as a successful professional or as a rich entrepreneur and looks one day at his wife and decides that she is too old for him and that he deserves better. These stories that basically spring from a fear of death and from the need of wanting to be young again always remind me of a patient of mine who looked at her husband when he was about to leave with a younger woman and yelled: "Remember, you are going to die anyway." Unfortunately, her husband was not ready to listen to such a dreadful truth and left without even looking back. But going back to Helena, I quickly understood that her marriage was over and that our time together would be put to better use by trying to understand what had attracted my patient to such an unreliable and immature man. Therapy with Helena lasted several months because besides the bereavement issues I wanted to work on the projections she had made on her husband of issues that she had disowned. Helena told me that she had met her now ex-husband when she was 25 years old. Being from a Latin American country where children leave the family home much later than in the United States, Helena had been living until then with her parents and as a result independence was not one of her strengths. On the other hand, her husband was not only from a different cultural group but also had been brought up to become very independent. It was not surprising that both fell passionately in love with the opposite other. We feel attracted by what we lack. When they married Helena continued being the protected woman she had been when living under her parents' roof. While their son was growing up the husband had been the only breadwinner. Helena stayed home with the baby. Later, when their son started school Helena continued her role of caretaker with no professional ambitions whatsoever. Taking care of her family made her feel that she had a purpose in life and she did not feel the need to explore other goals, professional or otherwise. On the other hand, her husband started becoming more and more successful and was often away. If we look at this situation from the point of view that we choose others to act out our repressed shadow, Helena's husband was definitely filling out his role to perfection. Thanks to him, Helena did not feel the need to become independent and struggle with the outside world. He was doing it for both of them. On the other hand, Helena was personifying the dependency needs of both. But sooner or later our shadow will catch up with us so that we fulfill our life tasks. As Jung once pointed out, what we don't acknowledge about ourselves will one day become our fate. That day came when Helena's husband left and she had no choice but to become a more independent human being. Fortunately she regrouped fairly quickly from the loss of her marriage and completed an academic degree that helped her find a job. Gradually Helena stopped having debts with herself. Having no other options but to individuate from her husband, she felt more at peace with herself and able to enjoy life more deeply. We could say that in a way her divorce was the karma she had chosen to become a more evolved human being. What would be interesting to know is how her husband coped with his repressed dependency needs.

*L. Frey-Rohn cited in *Anger, Madness and the Daimonic* by Stephen a. Diamond

LOVE THY NEIGHBOR

I have always been attracted by spirituality. Where I grew up there was a small chapel a couple of blocks away from my house where I went to mass every Sunday. The interior was beautifully carved in dark wood and the altar was always decorated with white flowers. Although nobody in my family was religious, when I was a teenager I deeply enjoyed listening to the liturgical music sang by the monks. As time went by I stopped going to mass and my interest in religion became a spiritual quest. One of the conclusions I reached early on in my spiritual journey was that basically all roads lead to Rome. If I have to summarize in one sentence the main message of all my readings on this subject it would be to love our neighbor as we love ourselves and to treat others like you would like to be treated. This precept first appeared in the Jewish Bible in Leviticus 19:18, but we also find it in the Gospels of the New Testament. I have always found this precept intriguing. Is it really possible to love others like we love ourselves? Buddhism goes even further as to say that since we are all interrelated we need to love our neighbor as we love our only child. We should not forget that in a previous life our neighbor might have been our child, our mother or our father, and as a result if we mistreat our neighbor we might be mistreating our own family. Believing that our neighbors might have been our children puts us without a doubt in a bind, especially in the case where our neighbor is not someone that we particularly like. So what does it really mean to love our neighbor like we love ourselves? I have always struggled, and still do, with this spiritual teaching. While some people are easy to like and to love, others have a knack for bringing out the worse in us. So how can we like them, let alone love them? Besides, feelings are independent from our will and act in a way similar to our autonomic nervous system. Loving, like breathing or digesting food, is an autonomous process not under our conscious control. Life would be so much easier if we could command ourselves to love this or that other person. Instead of waiting for prince charming to appear, we could produce loving feelings for someone who has a good personality as well as all the qualities we would like to see in a mate. Unfortunately, life does not work that way and when we meet someone with whom we have no chemistry we are unable to produce it. So what is the meaning of this precept so extensively used in all religious doctrines? I believe a possible answer to this question lies in the exegesis of the word love. How was this word used by the religious leaders of that time? How should we interpret its meaning? One interesting clue, I think, is provided by the

Buddhist precept of loving your neighbor as your only child." When we think of the way we love our children, the first thing that comes to mind is our sense of responsibility for their wellbeing. Human babies are the most fragile of nature, needing the care of their caregivers for many more years than any other being on the planet. As such, our love for our children has a lot to do with our commitment to keeping them safe. In this respect I remember reading a long time ago an article on parenting. The author had a very interesting concept on how to parent our children. The article stated that the goal of parenting was not that our children should love us, but that we should be responsible parents. I think this is a very interesting statement that sheds light on the question of what it means to love our neighbor like we love our children. In this context love has to do not with feelings but with our responsibility towards others and our commitment towards their well-being. We don't necessarily need to like our neighbors. What we need to do is make sure that we act towards them with compassion. In other words, I believe that loving our neighbor has to do with human interconnectedness and empathy. Interconnectedness, a basic concept in many Eastern religions, means that our actions will necessarily affect others in one way or the other. If our actions towards our neighbor are based on compassion, the effect will be positive. On the other hand, if we do not act responsibly towards others, the results will be harmful for them, for us, and for the entire universe.

THE HOUSE HAS BURNT TO THE GROUND. NOW I CAN SEE THE SKY.

JAPANESE KOAN

For those of us who besides being professional women have invested a lot of energy in raising a family, the end of a marriage and the children moving out will leave us with a deep sense of void. No matter how dysfunctional the marriage, a breakup is always felt as an irretrievable loss. When we get married we all have the hope that our union will last and that we will enjoy our grandchildren with the partner we have selected for life. Furthermore, our family is the refuge we have built through the years to shield us from life's hardships. When this partnership ends we are left alone, with no shelters to turn to, and with the harrowing task of moving into the unknown. I remember how Pat, one of my patients, whose husband had left the home after their last child started college, described this feeling to me during a session.

"It was a Sunday morning in early spring and the weather was lovely. I was writing emails in my study when suddenly a bird on a bush next to the window made a rustling sound. I looked up and saw the clear blue sky, the trees in bloom, the flowering bushes and all I could ask myself was: and now what?"

Life as she knew it had ended. A difficult task lay ahead of her: to pick up the pieces and start over. As Pat was talking to me I couldn't help but remember a Japanese koan I had come across in my readings of Buddhism. *The house has burnt to the ground. Now I can see the sky.* Her familiar life had burnt to the ground and had faced Pat with her ghosts and her repressed fears. When I told Pat that she needed to find a new purpose in life she looked at me in disbelief.

"A new life purpose? At my age? "

"I know it's difficult," I said. "But it can be done. It has to be done because with no purpose life becomes an empty shell."

Although not an easy task except for those people who have a definite calling, we all have talents that were relegated due to our many life duties in the first part of life. A friend of mine, I'll call her Sue, had always wanted to be an actress, but had never found the time to study acting. With two kids, a husband and work to make ends meet, acting had never been a priority. One day however, her sons left home to start their own lives and her husband followed them soon after. It was at that moment that Sue realized that the time had come for her to focus on her own life. The last years of her marriage had been plagued with lies, lack of communication, and boredom. Although Sue's first reaction to being suddenly left alone was a sensation of being surrounded by emptiness, she soon started taking acting lessons and gradually things in her life fell into place. Sue had found a new meaning to her life. But going back to Pat, "It's like being out in the woods", she explained to me during one of our sessions.

"I hear you," I said. "This is a new stage in your life and your old refuges are useless. You will have to find a new safe place for the person you are now." She agreed.

Several years have elapsed from that conversation and Pat has indeed overcome her post-divorce emptiness. After grieving for a couple of years for her past losses, she decided to enroll in a philosophy program. The courses proved to be an excellent move. Not only did she start focusing on herself and materializing what had always been a life interest, but she was also able to make new friends who had her same interests. Middle age is not for the faint at heart. Life changes so deeply that it takes all the energy we are capable of to adjust. At middle age, loss and loneliness are the names of the game. Like Pat and Sue, we have to become master builders of new refuges that will last us until a new change will come along to burn them to the ground. It is the only way to face with dignity this bumpy road called Life.

THERE ARE NO FACTS, ONLY INTERPRETATIONS

F. NIETZSCHE

Without any doubts Nietzsche explains in this statement exactly why human relations are so complex. One of my patients, I will call him Sergio, told me during a session that he had decided to register in an internet dating site. Sergio, a 38 year old divorced man, had had difficulties meeting people with whom to start a new relationship. The internet appeared to be a good alternative to expand his social network. After choosing one of the best known sites, he completed his profile and downloaded a recent picture. This done, he dedicated his free time to read the profiles of women his age to find a date. After a couple of days he finally found a lady (I will call her Amelia) that seemed appealing, not only physically. Amelia had stated in her profile that she worked in Sergio's same professional field, like him she had an only son, and was of his same generation. Without hesitation Sergio sent Amelia an email asking her if she was interested in knowing more about him. Her answer came almost immediately. Amelia said that she would like to communicate by email and, eventually, meet in person. That is how both started exchanging daily emails, without any urge to make an appointment to meet.

"It's very strange," Sergio told me once in session. "I have the feeling that I have known this woman forever. I am always looking forward to her messages".

After three weeks of email exchanges, Sergio made the suggestion of meeting Amelia personally. She agreed and they decided to meet at a bar after office hours. Since the date was still three days away, Sergio and Amelia kept writing to each other daily. One afternoon, two days before their appointment, Amelia sent Sergio an email to let him know that she wouldn't be able to make it because her son had injured himself during baseball practice. She had no one to take care of him but herself. She ended the message by saying that she was very sorry but that hopefully they would keep in touch. Despite feeling very disappointed, Sergio wrote to her saying that he totally understood the situation and told her not to worry. Then he came to session. I could tell that he felt more depressed than usual. Our first session had taken place three months prior when he came to see me due to his hopelessness and his difficulty with meeting people. When he met Amelia through the internet, the expectation of seeing her had brightened his mood significantly. Now, after her last email, sadness and loneliness had come back with a vengeance.

"I think this is a good opportunity to analyze the way you react to life frustrations", I said. That day Sergio looked gloomier than ever.

"I had a lot of expectations because from the way she wrote to me, I could tell that she has a nice personality," was Sergio's answer.

"I hear you. But life is messy, and if each time things don't go your way the ceiling caves in, you will live in a constant state of depression," I said.

"But how am I going to feel optimistic if she didn't even tell me that we could meet at a future time?" he whispered. "It's obvious that she has been playing games with me and that she has lost interest," he added with irritation.

"How do you know that she lost interest? Did she tell you so?" I asked.

"No, but at no time did she mention a future date."

"How do you know how she feels at this time? With her concerns about her son's wellbeing, her date with you is not a priority right now. Your thoughts are based on your interpretation of these facts, not on real facts. Can you see that?"

"Yes, but what is the alternative? What can I do?"

"Start by asking her if your date is still a given. If you don't ask her that question, all your interpretations are mere speculations."

"Yes, but she could tell me that we will meet when her son feels better and still be lying to me. In that case I wouldn't know the facts either."

"If she lies to you, you will probably be able to tell."

"How?"

"You'll know. We only believe those lies that we want to believe."

Sergio did not seem convinced.

"You are interpreting the present based on your past experiences. If you are able to discard the past and approach the present with an open heart, you will be able to have with others a more genuine relationship," was my answer.

Footnote: Years later Sergio came to see me to let me know that he had finally met Amelia and that after a year they had married. However, since the first day he met her Sergio was under the impression that Amelia was too beautiful and too intelligent to fall in love with him. Needless to say, this false impression never left him and generated innumerable and unnecessary conflicts in the marriage. As a result of Sergio's self-fulfilling prophecy Amelia did fall out of love and the marriage collapsed. Sergio's interpretation of facts had nothing to do with reality, but unconsciously he had to prove to himself that he was right. After the marriage was over Sergio finally understood his mistake. Unfortunately it was too late to make amends.

FAMILY THERAPY OR KARMA?

Like I have already mentioned a couple of times, I am a family therapist. For those of you who are not familiar with family therapy, one of the tenets of this psychological orientation is that in looking for a partner in life we look for familiar behavior patterns. That is why most of the time children of alcoholics will end up marrying alcoholics. Human beings are usually not comfortable with new situations; most of us prefer the known paths and the familiar ways of relating to others. That is what A. Napier and C. Whitaker meant when they stated that in order to marry the familiar often we end up marrying our worst nightmares.* The attraction to what is familiar is so strong, say family therapists, that even if the person we are attracted to is our worst option we will still fall in love. Only when catastrophe strikes us, some of us make our way into a therapist office to start the path towards individuation. According to theory, this is the only way to find the right partner next time around. But this is the psychological angle. If we move on and leave behind the phenomenological reality with all its theories and paradigms to enter the realm of metaphysics, our lives can be explained in a different manner. I am referring specifically to the concept of *karma*, or the concept of *dao*, which is the path that we need to follow in this life in order to become wiser. I have already shared with you my belief that we come to this life to learn, but only each one of us knows what the lesson will be. Georgina, a patient of mine, is a perfect example of what I am talking about. Some thirty years ago Georgina was living in a South American country and working as a translator for a well-known publishing house. One day, at the end of her workday, she was waiting downstairs for a friend to pick her up for dinner when suddenly a red car parked in front of the building. A young man stepped out of the car and as he entered the building he looked at Georgina intently. She returned his gaze and that was all it took for both of them to fall desperately in love at first sight. The attraction was mutual and they soon started going out and spending all their free time together. After almost a year of being together, Georgina's boyfriend decided that he wanted to come to the United States to study at a well-known university. So after he was accepted as a student they both decided that he would leave ahead of her and that she would join him later.

They were separated for eight months but kept always in touch by snail mail (since this story took place the 80s, email was non-existent at the time.) It was a very exciting time for both of them, especially because letters have a romantic quality that emails lack. While her boyfriend was gone Georgina was offered a better position in the company so she started working for a different publication. On the first day she started working at her new job she met a male colleague with whom she established a great friendship. At the time, he was in a situation very similar to hers: he was about to get married and move to another country to study abroad. This young man had all the things Georgina liked in a man: he was intelligent, friendly, handsome, sensitive and, most of all, humble. Georgina told me that she remembered asking herself at the time why was she not attracted to him who was in so many ways more similar to her than her actual boyfriend. Not only were they born in similar social backgrounds but religion was also the same. Not that she was a religious person, but religion has to do with culture and belonging to the same culture is a significant factor in marriage. Although Georgina and this man never went out on a date, on one occasion he invited her to a concert in a park, and when she declined he became upset. The fact that he became upset surprised her, but she was so much in love at the time that she did not give it a second thought. Time went by and they both left the country to pursue their separate life paths. After a couple of years of Georgina being married and living in the United States, this man called her to let her know that he was in her town and that he would like to see her and her husband. His call made her very happy and she promptly invited him to dinner. The three of them had a great time together remembering old times. He then called again several times even when Georgina and her husband moved to another city in the United States, and was always invited to dinner to their house. On one of those occasions he disclosed to her that he had named his daughter Georgina. At that time Georgina had already being married for several years and married life was not what she had expected. Her husband came from a very different background and living together was all but easy. The familiar echo that Georgina had found in him at first sight was his similarity with her mother, especially in his disproportionate sense of entitlement. Between them, she said, there were no negotiations or concessions. His opinion almost always prevailed. However, since she came from a very conservative family, Georgina kept going desperately trying to save a marriage that was already dead. Then one day her husband told her that her friend was killed in an accident. While in session with me she could still remember the anguish and the feeling that something very precious to her was lost. She also remembered that once long ago, while they were talking about a common friend who had aged prematurely, her friend had looked at her and said: "That is not going to happen to us."

"Was that a premonition? she asked me. "What did he mean? Did he think before dying that both of us should have been together instead of married to people who were not for us?"

"There are no definite answers to these questions," I answered. "As for me, I believe that such was your karma in this life and that you had no options. I believe that the strong attraction you felt for your ex-husband had more to do with you having to learn some lessons in this life that with the theories of family therapy. The taste of the familiar was only the hook. You were probably not ready for a more functional relationship just yet."

"True," agreed Georgina. But not everything is lost. Today I have my memories and the lessons learned. I also have a picture of my friend taken in my house that I have framed and placed with pictures of other dear friends. I also have a vivid dream of him coming to my room and kissing me tenderly. The only thing I am sure however is that the next time he asks me to a concert I will definitely go."

* *The Family Crucible*. A. Napier & C. Whitaker

THE SECRET OF LIFE IS NOW

Approximately a year ago I started writing a blog with the purpose of helping myself and others understand and overcome the many challenges life has in store for us, especially at middle age. Since I am a therapist, in most of the posts I wrote about life situations brought to my office by my patients, mostly middle age women, who after a life of being married and raising children were facing the challenge of being alone. Since that was also my life situation at the time, I sometimes wrote a post about my own life experience because I know that reading autobiographies is always captivating. I hope that my psychoanalytic colleagues will not feel too insulted by my self-disclosures. In my own defense I would like to mention the fact that several studies have shown that self-disclosure by therapists, when it has to do with the issue at hand and is appropriate, can benefit patients significantly. The life experience I would like to share with you all now has to do with the real Secret of Life. In other words, the magic formula that will help us live with serenity and without that feeling of always falling off a cliff. Cliffs appear when life presents us with change. Being as we are creatures of habit, changing jobs, moving to another country, or changing social status, will generate in us feelings of anxiety and can even cause panic attacks. When all of a sudden our known world crumbles and all that is familiar to us caves in like a house of cards, we are suddenly confronted with a no man's land with no maps and no points of reference to guide us. Therefore, what awaits us is the mysterious task of facing ourselves in loneliness. Although we all have the inner resources to do it, it is easier said than done. We need to remember that the way we approach this task will disclose to us, or not, the Secret of Life. But going back to my own experience, after thirty years my marriage went to pieces. Perhaps the main reason being that when children leave home and the couple stops being a triangle to become a dyad, very often the intimacy, the complicity and the communication between partners are not there any longer and it's difficult to recuperate them. In my particular case I tried to do the best I could to put the pieces of my marriage back together but failed. The years that followed were not the hardest of my life but were sufficiently difficult to make me understand that if I wanted to have a life, I needed to make some changes. Either that or stay forever stuck in the past. I had no options. I didn't really know where to start; what I did know was that whatever I did, I would not be able to do it by meditating and emptying my mind of thoughts. Quite the contrary, I had the feeling that I had to think and think some more to be able to understand the meaning of what had happened in my life. Those were years of deep introversion, with a question following another question, with very few convincing answers and almost no shelters to keep me safe. Those were also years of reading precious books again with the hope of finally finding the magic formula that would change my life forever. Two, three, five years went by without any results until one day something amazing happened. If I had to compare it to something it would be to those near death experiences where people who have been resuscitated speak about a marvelous feeling of being at peace and of everything being right. That evening I had met a friend for dinner. We started talking about how difficult it is for middle age women to find a suitable partner due to the importance Western society confers to youth and beauty. Some women even talk about feeling "transparent", meaning by this that nobody even looks at them anymore. While we were talking about this subject, my friend brought up an event from my marriage and very inappropriately asked me if I didn't regret it. My answer was that I didn't because if I had acted in a certain way it was because my unconscious had probably induced me to do so to protect me. Let's not forget that our unconscious is our link to Divinity and will always guide us where we need to go. I don't remember feeling irritated by my friend's words. I simply did not pay attention to her comments anymore. That is, my conscious mind didn't; my unconscious did. That night I dreamt that *I wanted to get into my house but did not find the key. The dream was not anxiety provoking; on the contrary. What I thought was: "How strange, I never lose anything. I must be changing."* But what was really surprising was waking up. The following morning for the first time in many years I felt a deep sense of joy as well as a feeling of relief for not being any longer in the difficult circumstance that had been the last years of my marriage. I finally felt that I had stopped missing the past and that I had lost the keys to the jail I had built in my own mind. I was changing. I had started accepting my current reality which is the only one I have and which, if I look really closely, is full of blessings. From that miraculous day on, I regained the ability to enjoy the little things in life: a shared meal, the chats on the beach, the view of the sea, a job well done, being in good health, and most of all, having family and friends near. I finally understood what Eckhart Tolle means when he talks about *The Power of Now*. Now I see that when we are stuck in the past we are unable to learn the lessons that will make us wiser. Yes. As you might have guessed, the Secret of Life means to throw away the keys to the past and to accept the fact that we are precisely there where we need to be.

∞